W9-AHL-590

THE
OLD
RUSH

MARKETING FOR GOLD
in
THE AGE OF AGING

THE
OLD
RUSH

MARKETING FOR GOLD
in
THE AGE OF AGING

PETER HUBBELL

LONDON   NEW YORK   SHANGHAI
MADRID   BARCELONA   BOGOTA
MEXICO CITY MONTERREY   BUENOS AIRES

Published by
LID Publishing Inc.
420 Round Hill Road
Greenwich, CT 06831
info@lidpublishing.com
www.lidpublishing.com

A member of:

BPR
Business Publishers Roundtable

www.businesspublishersroundtable.com

Printed in the United States
ISBN: 978-0-9852864-6-0

Cover designer: Bina Santos
Text designer: Laura Hawkins
Copy editor: Ellen Greenblatt
Proofreader: Debra Rhoades

TABLE OF CONTENTS

FOREWORD
By Jane Pauley

BOOMERS TODAY

We live in remarkable times. This is the first time that it is likely that you can be sixty years old and still feel that you can be productive; that you matter. In previous generations – all with exceptions that prove the rule – to arrive at this age meant you no longer mattered and that it was time for you to "leave the stage." Baby Boomers are aging into a unique, fortuitous moment in the history of the world when you can be fifty and still plan what you want to do next.

In fact, the ages of fifty or sixty can now look aspirational to younger people. If, for example, you are in your early forties and have a job that is not all that fulfilling but have to keep at it to support your children, you might look forward with anticipation to reaching an age where you can pursue a more rewarding, if not necessarily more lucrative, line of work.

Boomers are the first generation to get a heads-up when they are approaching "retirement age," that there are additional opportunities available, if they want to seize them. Boomers are also likely to be the last generation to consciously confront the issue of reimagining themselves in order to keep being productive after the traditional career arc. The generations that follow will just assume that reinvention is a normal stage at that age, and at many other ages.

As someone who has had a lifelong fascination with how lives get led, I am intrigued by how people are navigating these new life transitions. In order to understand what's happening, I have collected the stories of Boomers who have reimagined themselves. Thirty-three of these stories are featured in my book *Your Life Calling: Reimagining the Rest of Your Life* (New York: Simon & Schuster, 2014).

While writing this book I discovered that the secret of reimagining one's life is that there isn't just one secret: each of the thirty-three stories is unique and different. My hope is that for any given reader, something in one of the stories will spark something in you that will make you more open to ideas about who you are, where you come from, what skills you have, what has made you happy and what hasn't. Once you have done this thinking and your antennae are up, you'll be ready to recognize an opportunity if it comes into your field of vision.

During my research for the book, it became clear that reimagining one's life is often a process that is full of surprises. Some people who initially thought that they wanted a traditional retirement of relative leisure found out that they were much happier working. Some who thought of themselves as "white collar" types found pleasure and fulfillment getting their hands dirty. Almost no one charted a path and followed it.

There was, however, one question that almost all of the successful Boomer re-imaginers that I had the pleasure to meet answered in the same way. When I asked them if they could have performed the feat of reimagining themselves when they were thirty or forty, they said, "absolutely not." Their ability to reimagine themselves was built by their life experiences. It was a capability that came with maturity.

One problem that I have bumped up against while talking and writing about what we Boomers are doing as we age is that we don't yet have the right vocabulary to describe the phenomenon. For example, we use the word "retirement" to refer to what happens when someone leaves a traditional work setting after many years. But the vast majority of the people leaving those workplaces are planning to keep working. We need some new words.

While I have been looking at how individuals have been navigating these new realities, Peter Hubbell has been looking at how the cumulative effects of all the individual decisions are changing the shape of markets and business opportunities. Our starting points and approaches are different, but we share the basic perspective that the greatest impact of the Boomer generation is still to come. As someone who prefers to think forward rather than backward, I can't wait to see what we do.

PREFACE

I've always wanted to write a book. Gene Hackman once said that life is one long interruption between what you intended to do but never got around to doing. So much for good intentions.

If I was to write a book, what I needed was a deadline, for at the rate I was going, I was at risk of being dead before I published a single line. As the founder and CEO of BoomAgers, a modern communications company dedicated to Baby Boomers and aging, I knew that in a year, something special was going to happen. If timing is everything, 2014 was to be my deadline. I would finally get around to doing what I had always wanted to do.

I've often joked that the only way I was able to become a CEO was by starting my own company. Now it seemed that the only way I was going to succeed at being a credible CEO was to write a book. I needed some real inspiration, and one of the obvious first places to look was at our own business and our biggest challenges. I noted that the most challenging part of BoomAgers' success has been the need to perpetually evangelize a business opportunity that seemed so obvious to us that we thought it should have been selling itself.

You see, the Baby Boomers are the largest, wealthiest segment in the history of marketing, and while they still dominate almost all product categories, marketers have been slow to embrace an older consumer whom they judge to be less valuable than a younger one. If one believes in the power of advertising – and I must – then a book would be the perfect way to advertise our compelling point of view. Marketing to Boomers, I reckoned, was like fishing in the bathtub, and my book would be the invitation to go on a successful fishing expedition. (I may not have been at all biased by my lifelong passion for fishing.)

More objective minds encouraged me to find a new metaphor. Eureka! We arrived at the Gold Rush. In a day and age where fast growth is the new imperative, every company is looking to dig for gold where no one else is. With the Boomer cohort being so valuable, and literally undiscovered in marketing, we had found a new way to advertise the opportunity: The Old Rush.

I've always advised others that if you want to be really good at something, you need to focus on something you're really passionate about. After years of not writing a book, I have found writing this book to be an absolute joy because I so steadfastly believe in its statement and purpose.

I have been blessed with a wonderful career in advertising that has offered me experiences that this farm boy never could have imagined. This book is but one of the responsibilities I feel to share my wisdom and know-how with others who have the open minds that creative marketing demands.

So come stand with me in the mighty river of marketing and pan for gold. In our search for the next big idea, we will have to sift through a lot of gravel, but our mutual passion will lead us to the real nuggets. I know our quest will be successful, for if this book merely inspires you, you will be richer for the experience.

Finally, I am grateful for having grown up on a farm, where I learned the value of hard work; for Tim Love, the best man in Advertising, for teaching me how to work; for John Bowman, my lifelong business partner, who has always been a joy to work with, and for my dear wife Caroline and family, who give my work purpose.

Special thanks on this project also go to Andrew Frothingham for his editorial contributions, and to Michael Tive, who provided essential wisdom and the daily carrot and stick needed for this endeavor to see the light of day.

PETER B. HUBBELL

INTRODUCTION

What is the next big thing? That's the one question that marketers ask most. Marketing is an opportunistic business, and success usually depends on identifying the hottest trend of the moment and getting to market first. Since none of us has a crystal ball, we must rely on intelligence and instinct to help us predict the next big move in the marketplace.

Typically, the next big thing has been an emerging medium or an emerging market; said another way, technology or geography. Once these opportunities manifest themselves, marketing's version of a gold rush soon ensues. Witness the race to figure out the newest way to do social media better or the rush to expand beyond India to Indonesia and sub-Saharan Africa. Marketers love "new."

But wait a moment. If a tree falls in the woods and there is no one there to hear it, does it make a sound? None of these enticing new trends matter without people to consume the products and services that marketers market. If nothing is more important than consumers, why doesn't the search for the next big thing ever begin with them?

It should. In fact, the next big thing is a consumer thing. It's also really big, and it's already here.

January 1, 2014, marked not the beginning of another new year, but the beginning of a new era: the Age of Aging. This is the year that the last of the eighty million Baby Boomers will turn fifty and officially graduate from marketing's coveted eighteen to forty-nine target audience. The Boomers aren't just another generation passing through time – they are the

Most Valuable Generation™. Their influence on our culture and the marketing landscape has been both dramatic and unprecedented, and the power of their numbers and wealth will continue to transform the world around them even as they age.

In less than five years, 50% of the U.S. adult population will be fifty and older and they will spend close to $3 trillion dollars a year, up 45% from the prior decade. They also dominate 94% of Consumer Packaged Goods (CPG) product categories and spend 50% of CPG dollars.

Aging is also a global trend. People sixty-five and over will soon outnumber children under five for the first time in world history. Consumers sixty and over in China outnumber the entire population of Russia. When the fixation on debt in countries like Greece, Italy and Spain gives way, it will reveal a deeper economic woe – the impact of aging on the size of the active workforce and on the tax revenue it produces. This is the Age of Aging, and no other trend will do more to impact global public policy and human welfare.

If this is compelling, then this book is the first step toward realizing the opportunity. Think of *The Old Rush* as a heads-up, a bit of a *pssst* to help turn you on to the opportunity that has the power to turn businesses around overnight. The book is built around the metaphor of the Gold Rush, and it is a rich one.

Part One grounds us in the history of the Baby Boomer generation, from birth to current day. Boomers were born into unprecedented times in unprecedented numbers, and the context in which they lived formed personal values that continue to influence their behavior and brand choices. This section also speaks to the powerful myths and misconceptions that have left most marketers blind to the massive opportunity at hand.

Part Two develops the Gold Rush metaphor and shares lessons to be learned from the original Gold Rush of 1849. The Gold Rush presented incredible and irresistible potential, but it took a unique breed of person to prevail over the adversity that stood between the dream and actual success. Those who packed up and acted first were the original "first movers." When they got to California they found gold on the ground. Those who waited to follow dug harder and deeper for smaller nuggets. The Old Rush is the next chance to strike it rich in marketing.

Finally, Part Three offers up practical, modern-day advice for succeeding in this marketing opportunity. The insights that are shared reflect the real-world experiences of BoomAgers, a modern communications company dedicated to Boomers and Aging, and founded by the author. Like the Gold Rush itself, marketing to Boomers is not a stroll in the park. There are right ways to do it and wrong ways. The final section of this book is the map that will guide you safely and successfully on your quest for gold in the Age of Aging.

In its totality, this book is meant to be informative, inspiring and, hopefully, entertaining. It draws on knowledge from history and the invaluable experience of the author's thirty-two years on Madison Avenue. If its purpose is served, it will encourage more and better marketing innovation directed at a generation that still deserves the best that brands have to offer.

In closing, seek some inspiration from one of the most memorable lines in American cinema. What Boomer could forget *The Graduate* (1967) and the classic scene in which Dustin Hoffman (as Ben Braddock) is offered career advice by Mr. McGuire, who tells him that the future is "plastics." Movie viewers laughed this one off, but look at plastics now. If you were smart enough to have gotten into the business then, you would have struck it rich on molded gold ten times over. The Old Rush? It's your chance to get to the future first. The Boomers are the future. Think about it, and read on.

PART
ONE
COMING OF AGE

CHAPTER
═══ ONE ═══

BOOM! PEACE, OPTIMISM
AND BABIES
A new generation comes to life.

All too often, we try to understand people by measuring them in the moment. We wonder why they acted in a certain way. What were they thinking? What now? In marketing, many of the answers lie in understanding basic human motivations, but we seldom look back far enough to understand the influence of values developed in one's formative years. The Boomers were born into an unprecedented set of circumstances that explain why they behaved the way they did then and how they behave now. To understand them going forward, we must start by going backward.

After four dread-filled years of conflict, the explosions of World War II eventually gave way to peace and a different kind of explosion – a global population boom. As the uncertainty of war faded, plans for the future grew brighter and families grew bigger.

In the years prior to the war, the number of births per year in the U.S. tended to hover between two and three million. During the post-war years of 1951 to 1953, that number climbed above three million on its ascent to four million during 1954 to 1964. When the full effect of peace and

GOLD
NUGGETS

THE GENERATION GUIDE[1]

The Greatest Generation
1901–1924

The Silent Generation
1925–1945

The Baby Boomers
1946–1964

Generation X
1965–1976

Millennials/Generation Y
1977–1995

Generation Z
1996→

prosperity was realized, the U.S. had added nearly eighty million new residents, the greatest population boom in our country's history.

This incredible number of babies born between the years of 1946 and 1964 was aptly coined the "Baby Boomers", a new generation that dramatically altered the demographic balance of the country. The combined effect of adding millions of new babies at a time when we had lost a significant number of adults in the war meant that the U.S. suddenly had many more youngsters in proportion to adults than in years gone by.

Chances are that you are familiar with these facts and events, as they have been the focus of extended reporting over the years. Comparatively less attention, however, has been given to the unique circumstances into which this massive generation was born, circumstances that help bring understanding as to why the Baby Boomers behaved as they did as youngsters and why they behave the way they do now.

While this new generation was influenced by a broad and complex array of societal factors, the circumstances that had the most defining impact on it were freedom, optimism, prosperity and destiny.

With the end of the war came new beginnings. The American spirit had shown itself to be as irrepressible as ever, and as the grip of war relinquished its hold, the country and its people were suddenly free again. Freedom had restored their ability to live their lives as they wished, and when freedom flourishes, prosperity is usually not far behind.

Freedom was felt by all, but for those returning from war there was also personal pride. The veterans, most now new fathers, rejoiced in the fact that they had acted together to accomplish something pretty remarkable. They had defeated sinister enemies, shown the world our resolve, and saved our American way of life. They had a sense that they could do anything, and they even had a genuine hero to lead the way. Dwight D. Eisenhower, a victorious general and reassuring, fatherly figure, was now president. The country that believed it could do anything was brimming with optimism.

Both optimism and the economy flourished. To fuel the war effort, the U.S. had built a massive industrial infrastructure that was still intact and now available for domestic commerce. In contrast, most of the infrastructure of the battle zone countries had been destroyed. With most of Europe and Asia struggling to rise from their rubble, the U.S. quickly and easily rose to dominate the world's markets. This economic momentum continued as the U.S. had the wealth, the will, the sense of destiny and the leadership to keep expanding its infrastructure.

In 1956, President Eisenhower signed The Federal-Aid Highway Act to initiate the building of our country's interstate highway system. At the time, it was the largest public works initiative ever undertaken in this country. The once-general saw the highways as essential to defense mobilization. While Ike also knew that they would foster economic development, it's unlikely that he could have fully anticipated the profound change that interstate highways would have on how and where people lived in America.

Then secretary of defense Charles Erwin Wilson, formerly the head of General Motors, was very influential in the planning of the interstate system. Not surprisingly, Detroit was revving up to take advantage of the broad demand for automobiles that a national highway system would create.

The population was already booming, but the rate of car ownership would soon rise even faster. In 1945, there were some 222 cars for every 1,000 Americans. As the parents of Boomers busied themselves buying family automobiles, the number of cars per 1,000 rose to 324 in 1956 (one of eight were station wagons). The car trend was only just getting started. In 1960, the number hit 410, and by 1970, when the Boomers themselves started to get driver's licenses, the number reached 545 per 1,000. Soon, continued Boomer driver demand helped drive the number up to 844 in 2007, nearly one car per person.

America wasn't simply building highways and selling cars, it was creating mobility. This was the original, wireless mobile society. Almost overnight, the automobile had liberated people from streetcars and their overhead wires and limited routes. Now one was free to drive almost anywhere, at any time.

The soldiers who returned from the war returned from another part of the world. They had experienced and survived places their parents had never been, and now had the confidence and willingness to live farther from home. They were different and more mobile than their parents. They craved newness and yearned to raise their precious babies, their icons of the bright future, in enclaves safe from the dangers they associated with the cities of their childhoods. The growth of highways and the proliferation of pavement provided easy access to more distant areas. The first ones to get there were the real estate developers.

The real estate developers had sensed post-war families' hunger for homes of their own, so they began to build the suburbs. Modern, affordable communities (a new word at the time), filled with adorable, affordable homes – just enough privacy, good schools close by and a postage stamp lawn to keep green and well cut. One of the most iconic suburbs was Levittown, New York, or, to be more accurate, the

Levittowns. The first to capitalize on the Baby Boom, Levitt & Sons were pioneers in building planned communities using mass production methodologies. The houses may have been mocked by folksingers as being "ticky-tacky," but their newness and affordability proved irresistible, and a new way of living was spawned.

Highways weren't the only element of our infrastructure that promoted freedom and mobility – consider the impact of air travel. During and after the war, our domestic aviation capabilities (again in the interest of national defense) grew rapidly. The technology (then called "know-how") that had been developed to make and move materials for the war was ready for peacetime application. Returning veterans had experienced air travel, and suddenly flying was a little less scary and perhaps even enjoyable. It was time to "fly the friendly skies" of United. Transportation expanded on the land, in the skies and also on the sea, as ports developed for the war became thriving departure points for cruise ship adventures.

While the war had raged, it was everyone's patriotic duty not only to be as productive as possible but also to create flawless products. Omnipresent posters reminded everyone that being lazy at work and at home could cause soldiers to die abroad. This commitment to productivity, quality and innovation continued after the war and gave rise to new categories of consumer products that offered new kinds of convenience. By 1949, a harried mother who used to make scratch cakes could make dessert faster with a Betty Crocker cake mix. If she was truly done in, she could simply buy a ready-made Sara Lee Cheesecake.

At the same time, manufacturers began to think a lot more about the consumers who were going to use their products. It was no longer a matter of making what you had always made and then handing it off to a salesman or a shopkeeper who would try to sell it. Increasingly, the approach was to find out what the consumer needed or wanted and then to manufacture to those specifications. This shift in thinking, coupled with the new logistical capabilities that let a company distribute differing sets of products to different kinds of stores in different geographies, led to the birth of modern marketing.

Modern marketing was born alongside the Baby Boom. No one understood the impact of this as it happened, but there were a few phenomena that hinted at the size of the changes that were to come. In 1954, at the peak of the Baby Boom, the American Broadcasting Company (ABC) aired five, one-hour *Disneyland* episodes of "Davy Crockett". The material was edited into a couple of theatrical-release movies and then aired on the National Broadcasting Company (NBC) in "living color" (remember the peacock?). Not long after the show had aired, a million coonskin caps were sold so that kids could look like their hero. Modern merchandising was also about to boom.

The America that sprouted after World War II was amazing in a host of ways. The country set new standards for the world with incredible production capacity, prosperity and energizing optimism applied to a modern infrastructure and a growing population. Many would contend that the country has yet to and might never again host such fertile conditions for sustained, long-term economic expansion.

While these conditions have not persisted, the greatest and most influential development of this period was the creation of the Baby Boom generation. What makes this generation so distinctive is not merely its size, but also the unique circumstances in which it grew. Baby Boomers grew up bathed in peace, optimism and prosperity, with unrestricted freedom to express themselves and to make their own choices.

As much of their world grew up with them, Boomers often had the sense that the world was made for them, in response to their wishes. To a large degree, they were right. As they were empowered to say and do what they wanted, businesses soon learned to listen to them, and the smartest ones learned how to follow their lead. Post-war society was being shaped by the post-war economy, which in turn was shaped by the demands of the Boomer consumer.

The Boomers were born into an unprecedented set of circumstances that led to new behaviors and formed new personal values. Whereas previous generations were raised to be more accepting of the circumstances that they inherited, the Boomers were empowered to change them. As they began to age, adolescent Boomers soon encountered another new circumstance – the need to distinguish themselves from their parents and to actively shape the world to their own specifications.

CHAPTER
═══ TWO ═══

IT'S 1969. DO YOU KNOW
WHERE YOUR KIDS ARE?
The Baby Boom babies are growing up.

While America was enjoying peacetime prosperity, the Baby Boomers were growing up quickly. Soon they had become teenagers, and for those of you who have raised your own teenagers, just imagine what it was like for one country to raise eighty million teenagers. These eighty million teenage Boomers were being raised during an increasingly controversial age. They searched for the meaning of life and shaped the lives of the country at the same time.

If a filmmaker were to put together a highlight reel of America circa 1969, it might include Bob and Carol and Ted and Alice canoodling on the big screen, or the cast of *Oh! Calcutta!* baring it all on Broadway, astronauts on the moon, Peter Max's pop art, a commune and surely some antiwar protests. It would almost certainly feature young people listening to music and rolling in the mud at Max Yasgur's dairy farm in rural Bethel, New York. The Woodstock Festival, through the power of its imagery, would go on to be the one event that most defined, correctly or not, the spirit of this new generation.

With the benefit of today's terminology, another way to think of the dynamic of Woodstock would be as "the original flashmob." Today, the term "flashmob" usually describes a group of people spontaneously brought together by messages relayed on phones and mobile devices. The cell phones and tablets don't create the flashmob – they're merely coordinating devices. What creates the flashmob is some fundamental human desire to become part of something that will provide pleasure and, ideally, bestow momentary social status. Defined in this way, Woodstock was not a pre-orchestrated protest statement, it was simply a talent-stocked summer music festival. As word got out, no self-respecting music lover wanted to be left out, and their fanaticism drew them to Bethel in hordes.

Although pictures of the pilgrimage to Woodstock suggested that every eligible American of age was in attendance, it simply wasn't so. Joni Mitchell's lyrics came close to getting the number right, "by the time we got to Woodstock, we were half a million strong." If all 500,000 in attendance were Boomers, which was not true, only one out of every sixteen of the eighty million would have been there. Hardly a majority by any stretch, yet the F\festival had a major and lasting impact in shaping the public's perception of this new generation.

In retrospect, the events of 1969 seem less remarkable when you consider the challenge of so many teens maturing at the same time. Coming of age is almost always a tumultuous time for anyone – in any American's life. This was the coming of age of an extraordinary number of people at the same time.

Smart marketers never take things as they are or as they seem. They must be incessantly curious and must keep penetrating a subject or phenomenon until they get to a pithy, vital understanding of its true motivation or essence. Behind most social or personal phenomena, there are timeless themes at work. Great advertising tends to consist of these timeless themes expressed in timely ways. For Woodstock, the timeless driver was the fact that teenagers crave a sense of belonging and are often eager to join in. Woodstock's promise of "Peace, Love and Music" also appealed to youth's hedonistic side.

Similarly, the activism that defined the 1960s was also inspired by a timeless motivation. Recall that the term that described activist events was "demonstrations." Although the term became synonymous with protests, it was a very apt term, as these demonstrations were actually demonstrations of the Boomers' values. If you consider that it's often easiest to demonstrate what you stand for by demonstrating what you stand *against*, these events became the best way for Boomers to express how important their values were to them.

Students at Kent State showed that they would risk, and in some cases lose, their lives for their values. For the most part, values that are defined during one's formative years seldom go away. They may manifest themselves differently during different life stages, but the core values that the Boomers formed during their youth still influence their choices today.

To more clearly understand the Boomers' values, you must look at them the way a Boomer would. Consider how the older generation might have judged the Boomers' values and choices using the goings-on of Woodstock as a barometer. Or what about their appearance? I will never forget joining my dad and his contemporaries on a fishing trip in the north woods in the 1970s. One of his older fishing buddies emphatically declared that all of the country's "problems" could be traced to the darn Beatles and their long hair.

Viewed through the eyes of an older generation, the Boomers' values often seemed confused or even self-contradictory. But to the Boomers themselves, there was nothing contradictory about joining a large crowd in order to express one's individuality.

GOLD
NUGGETS

By 2017
50% of U.S. adults will be fifty and over, and they will control 70% of the country's disposable income.

By 2030
the number of adults fifty and over will have increased by 34%.

By 2050
there will be 161 million consumers fifty and over in the U.S.

Baby Boomers
enjoy a per capita income that is 26% higher than the U.S. national average.

In 2012
fewer than 5% of all paid media spending in the U.S. targeted adults fifty and over.[2]

The Boomers in 1969, and the Boomers today, are more focused on their individual needs, wants and preferences than any earlier generation, which is a function of the world they were born into. Previous generations were born into subsistence economies where everyone had to pitch in to help the family get by. They weren't as likely to be oriented toward their own individual pleasure and well-being. As we have discussed, the Boomers grew up in an era of unprecedented prosperity. Everything was wonderful and almost everyone was optimistic. It was natural for them to have a tendency to focus on themselves.

As the leading-edge Boomers became adults, they weren't the only ones changing. The world around them was changing, and there were lots of question marks. The bottom started to fall out on prosperity, and corruption and malfeasance seemed to spread through government. Our foreign policies were questioned by many as the military was bogged down in the unpopular and seemingly unwinnable Vietnam War. The country's teens and new adults started to question the wisdom of the older generation and, with profound self-awareness, put their faith in their peers instead.

How did Boomers become so self-aware? In large measure, the Boomers' self-awareness was generated when the Boomers sensed that they had the ability to influence the world around them. Their sheer numbers made them a force at the polls and gave them critical leverage in chosen endeavors. However, the phenomenon that contributed most to their growing self-awareness was the fact that marketers were now making products for them, not just their parents.

Marketers' products broadly acknowledged Boomers' preferences, including items as basic as toothpaste, positioned to the Boomers early in their lives. Procter & Gamble (P&G) launched Crest toothpaste nationally in 1955, offering superior cavity prevention for young Boomers. In one of the notable marketing innovations of its time, Crest was formulated with stannous fluoride and sought the influential endorsement of the American Dental Association (ADA).

Crest's advertising campaign showed children returning from the dentist proudly exclaiming, "Look, Ma. No cavities!" The highly successful campaign made Boomers themselves the spokespeople and tacitly claimed that Crest was the toothpaste preferred by a new generation with new needs.

The Crest advertising slogan soon became part of the national vocabulary and even made its way into comic routines. The advertising campaign and a dedicated professional program aimed at dentists did their jobs. Crest grew past P&G's own Gleem toothpaste, and in October 1961, Crest moved past Colgate, the previous market share leader.

Boomers' parents often proved willing to buy what their darlings wanted, or what marketers said their children would want. The emergence of products custom-tailored for Boomers continued as Boomers earned their own money to spend on themselves.

Boomer demand drove fad after fad, often to the bewilderment of the Boomers' parents and teachers. Ask any Boomer about the fads they participated in while they were growing up, and you're in for a fun trip down memory lane. Duncan yo-yos were the rage in 1961, and again in various later years. Dances and songs like the Mashed Potato (1962), The Monkee (1963), The Hustle (1975) came and went. Twister, hula hoops, miniskirts, Nehru jackets, tie-dyed clothes, granny glasses, baseball cards, tops, mountain bikes, streaking, go-karts, pet rocks, mood rings and countless others.

Just as Woodstock was a flashmob, this attraction to fads was basically an early example of viral behavior. It wasn't like the Boomers all got together, had a meeting and agreed that the Beatles were cool. The word simply spread from Boomer to Boomer and soon there was a groundswell of Beatlemania.

As the Boomers continued to age, they did what most adolescents do: they rebelled against their parents and turned to their peers for companionship, validation and standards. They demonstrated their passion for judging everything from products to governments on the basis of their values. They moved the locus of authority from parents and society to the individual.

This focus on the individual flourished in all areas of Boomer life and remains a defining characteristic of this generation to this day. The Boomers have claimed the right to live and participate on their own, personal terms. They see it as their right and duty to evaluate all life options personally. The rationale "because it has always been done this way" has never meant much to them. If anything, encouraging them to embrace the status quo acts as an invitation to do things differently.

The Boomer adults of today were molded by the circumstances and context of their youth. This generation's sheer size alone – values not withstanding – would go on to amplify the impact of their choices even as their age and place in society changed. Strength in numbers was about to take on a whole new meaning.

CHAPTER
THREE

STRENGTH IN NUMBERS
Eighty million strong and making things happen.

"Amplification" is variously defined as either a "massive replication" or an "expanded statement." It would seem to be an apt word, given how often we have already used the words "massive" and "statement" to describe this generation. The adjective "massive" is also the source of the shorthand term "mass marketing." Mass marketing is fundamentally about amplification – that is, designing one message that can influence many. When mass marketing was targeted to a massive generation, the results were phenomenal. Never before had so much been at stake for so many American marketers.

As the Boomers began to really flex their muscles as consumers, they triggered the fads we spoke of earlier, but they also triggered more substantial and lasting trends, some of which have persisted until today. Time after time, the Boomers took something that appealed to their values, lifestyles and preferences and elevated it to near-iconic status.

Even though "amplification" is a marketing term now popularized in social media, it's a dynamic that has been there all along. It is what happens when a large number of people catch on to something at the same time. In traditional print, publishers called it "pass-along readership." In the modern web environment, it's called "going viral." Using today's terminology, Boomers made brands go viral, big time.

Witness the creation of a timeless fashion classic: blue jeans. Back in the days of Woodstock and before, the term "blue jeans" did not exist. They were known as "dungarees," and they were strictly for work and the working class. Few self-respecting adults would wear a pair into town or much less to a meeting. Dress codes prohibited the wearing of dungarees at many clubs, restaurants and schools, essentially anywhere outside of the workplace. Many adults who had office or managerial jobs didn't even own a pair of dungarees.

Today, it is hard to find an adult who doesn't have a pair of jeans. The social stigma once associated with wearing dungarees has been replaced by the style statement of wearing a great pair of jeans. The advent of "casual fridays" even legitimized wearing jeans in the workplace – a fashion practice that would have been unthinkable several decades before – to show that they are "regular folks." Many folks have even abandoned the idea of donning their starchy, scratchy "sunday best" outfits and now wear jeans to church. There are many more kinds of jeans today and many consumers have separate work jeans and dress jeans. How did this happen? Essentially, Boomers adopted the blue jean as the uniform of youthful proletarian rebellion and a fashion trend was born.

Dungarees had been around a long time. The Levi-Strauss Company was founded in San Francisco in 1853 and had been selling "durable pants" – also known as "waist overalls – since 1873. They were in limited distribution and were often found in outlets like an Army-Navy surplus store. A relatively obscure piece of clothing, their elevation to a fashion classic had little to do with availability and everything to do with demand and the demandingness of a large generation.

Boomers soon saw dungarees being worn by the movie

stars that they were adopting as heroes. James Dean, the star in *Rebel Without a Cause* in 1955, is a perfect example. Boomers instantly connected with Jim Stark, the sensitive, misunderstood character he portrayed and his sense of disconnection from his parents and authorities. They also loved Dean as Cal Trask in *East of Eden* and as Jett Rink in *Giant.* He was universally worshipped, and he always seemed to be in dungarees.

After Dean's dramatic, early death in a race car that bore his nickname, "Little Bastard," his legend grew. Boomers around the country plastered their bedrooms and dorm rooms with pictures and posters of Dean to show that they, too, were rebels. They studied his slouch and wore their dungarees exactly the way he did.

Even Boomers who weren't part of the James Dean cult embraced dungarees – now popularized as jeans – as a personal fashion statement. These were pants that signified solidarity with working people and offered up quiet criticism of more formal society. Societal institutions such as schools, clubs, stores and churches that wanted Boomers to show up had no choice but to loosen their dress codes. The wearing of jeans was no longer simply the choice of outliers, it was the choice of one of the most vital groups of society. For the institutions that had traditionally dictated the standards and norms of society, the shoe was now on the other foot of a jean-clad leg.

Naturally, it didn't take long before classic jeans became commoditized and marketers and Boomers alike began to seek a new take on jeans. They found a new fad in bell-bottom jeans.

Like the original dungarees, bell-bottomed jeans had their origin in the proletariat ranks, in this case sailors who needed a pant whose legs they could easily roll up to keep them dry while swabbing the deck. The new hip-hugging bell-bottoms – especially "elephant bells" – used extravagant amounts of fabric at the bottom of the legs to made an obvious statement. The swaying of the bells while sashaying down the street quickly became the new must-have look.

Another manifestation of unified Boomer power was the politically motivated battle cry, "Don't Trust Anyone over Thirty," coined by Jack Weinberg, now in his mid-sixties. While it was created and used by Boomers in their twenties for years, it stuck even as many of them turned thirty and older. In hindsight, this was the beginning of this generation's irrational sense of agelessness. Of course they knew that they were technically older than thirty – and not to be trusted themselves. Illogically, they rationalized that since they didn't act like they were thirty, the rule did not apply to them. Sound familiar?

As the Boomers were searching for the meaning of life, Madison Avenue found meaning in their magnitude. Both Coke and Pepsi aimed their marketing efforts squarely at the massive Boomer audience. They jousted for the rights to claim title as the Boomers' soft drink of choice. Coke had traditionally used imagery to appeal to Boomers while keeping their slogans broad enough to attract broad audiences. Then, in a departure, they famously used real Boomer language when they debuted "It's the Real Thing" in 1969. In 1971, they aired the iconic "I'd Like to Buy the World a Coke" mountaintop commercial, which went on to become an eternal Boomer anthem. The song was steeped in Boomer values. The peace and love of Woodstock were pleasantly, beautifully, liltingly, memorably extended to become "Peace, Love and Coke."

Pepsi fought back, often with slogans that staked explicit claims on youth and the youthful generation. From 1961 to 1964, they sang, "Now It's Pepsi for Those Who Think Young." Then from 1964 to 1967 they boldly sought to own the generation by asserting, "Come Alive, You're in the Pepsi Generation."

In each of the Pepsi and Coke commercials, music played a crucial, central role. Boomers have always insisted on having "their" music. For many years, Madison Avenue's music of choice was rock and roll because it was the format made popular by and preferred by Boomers.

Next came disco, which swiftly infiltrated the radio airwaves and the canned sound tracks in stores. Disco also brought with it a host of fashion trends, including platform shoes and double-knit (bell-bottom) pants.

The shift to disco from rock and roll seems at first like a substantial leap. Rock and roll was, by nature, rebellious and out of control. Disco had more conformity and control about it. It came with a new kind of dancing that required couples and orderly, in-line dance formations. But when you look more closely, with the deeper lens of looking for the motivations behind the behaviors, the arrival of disco made perfect sense.

Disco is perhaps best described as "giddy hedonism," and Boomers have always been hedonistic. Disco dancing, like dancing to rock, was a higher art of feeling good – über Boomer. Boomers never pretended to be puritanical. Their parents focused on practicality and survival, but the Boomers focused on self. They are a generation of pleasure seekers of the highest order.

The amplification effect also transformed the car business. Boomers may have professed a love for Mother Earth at Woodstock, but that allegiance was often no match for the

GOLD
NUGGETS

Over the course of the **next twenty years**,
the Baby Boomers will inherit
$15 trillion in cash and other assets.[3]

10,000 Baby Boomers turn
sixty-five every day and this will continue
for the **next seventeen years**.[4]

52% of U.S. adults
age fifty to sixty-four expect to
retire later than age sixty-five
and **25%** report that
they will **"never" retire**.[5]

pure hedonistic rush that you could get from driving a high-powered muscle car. When the Boomers made it clear that they wanted more horsepower, Detroit's car companies obliged. Boomers raced each other in gas-guzzling GTOs, Camaros, Gran Sports, Charger RTs, Road Runners and others.

When I was in high school, the students lucky enough to have a muscle car paraded them along the school driveway by day and raced the same road at night. I often wondered what must have crossed the school's mind when it designed a driveway that was a mile-long straightaway.

While I lived close enough to school that walking there each day would have been easy, the thought of arriving on foot was mortifying. My father walked miles to school and back in drifting snow (didn't everyone's dad?), but I would go to great lengths to make sure that I made my entrance on four wheels, if just as a passenger. That generally meant begging and bribing my brother to fit me in to "The Grey Bomb," a rotund '53 Chevy inherited from a neighboring farmer.

Our lives were consumed by doing whatever it took to come into ownership of a muscle car. Did all the power in these mean machines have a practical purpose? Rarely. Were they fun? Absolutely. The pattern held true: Boomers got what they wanted.

I will always associate the music of the time with the cars of the time. My brother had installed a state-of-the-art eight-track player in his Chevy, and it worked reasonably well as long as you wedged a matchbook into the front of the mechanism to force the cartridge into alignment with the tape head. Tapes were expensive, so we grew accustomed to playing the same "favorites" over and over again. Endless hours were spent listening to the Yes album *Tales from Topographic Oceans*, Rod Stewart, Bob Dylan and, toward the end of the eight-track era, some Aerosmith. This was our music. It belonged to us then, and it still does now. Gen Y is simply borrowing Steven Tyler from us. Dream on.

As stated, savvy marketers saw what was happening and responded with a proliferation of products. In areas where proliferation wasn't as easily accomplished, the needs and wants of the Boomers became paramount and squeezed other demographic groups out of the equation. This started to happen with media, and consequently with advertising.

Boomers have always had an enormous appetite for media, particularly broadcast media. Commercial radio stations across the nation began to change their rock and roll formats to facilitate selling Boomer audiences to advertisers. Television, with its more expensive and complex infrastructure, couldn't Boomerize as quickly, but it too steadily grew.

When the majority of the Boomers were young, most cities and towns were reached only by the three major networks, and one independent station. With limited content, the programming ran for only part of the day. With limited programming and typically just one television per home, families sat down together to watch shows like Walt Disney's *Wonderful World of Color* on a Sunday evening.

The business model that commercial television was built on involved creating audiences and selling them to advertisers. In order to set rates, the stations had audits performed on their audiences to measure their size. The audits broke the audiences down by age and gender and most often focused on the eighteen to forty-nine bracket. While a few shows such as Lawrence Welk's were sold for their ability to deliver older audiences, and others for audiences eighteen and younger, the eighteen to forty-nine demographic quickly became the sweet spot that most programming was created for. Hence, the television and marketing industries came of age embracing the idea that eighteen to forty-nine were the ages where the action was.

Over the years, television stations and programs proliferated, as did the number of TVs per household. CBS began broadcasting some programs in color in 1951, but few households had color TVs. Some cable networks such as MTV (launched in 1981) and VH-1 (launched in 1985) relied on their ability to reach younger audiences, including many viewers under eighteen. But for the most part, the dedication to the eighteen to forty-nine age bracket remained at the core of television marketing discussions. Why shouldn't it? As long as the Boomers populated this age bracket, their enormous purchasing power was squarely in the crosshairs of marketers and could make or break brands.

The way to get to the Boomer audiences that advertisers wanted was to broadcast programs that Boomers wanted to watch. So Boomers began to have enormous, if indirect, influence over what was broadcast over the public airwaves. This applied to advertising even more than it did to programming.

Boomers, for the most part, didn't set out to change the nature of our culture. It wasn't deliberate. Their agenda was much more individual and me-centric. They wanted what they wanted, when they wanted it and how they wanted it. The size of the Boomer demographic meant that individual decisions were aggregated into such large numbers that they triggered trends in every aspect of life. The Boomers didn't get what they wanted because they were using some sort of generational blackmail; they got what they wanted because it was almost always best business decision to give them whatever would most please them.

CHAPTER
FOUR

THE ORIGINAL BRAND MANAGERS
The advent of consumerism and branding.

As the Boomers grew older and made more money, marketers made it easier for them to spend that money on products and services that seemed essential. These were the wonder years for marketers – unprecedented population growth and prosperity combined with the advent of electronic media and expanded consumer credit. This was the cocktail that created Madison Avenue's Mad Men.

As stated, the Boomers had enjoyed an unusual childhood, a rebellious adolescence and more time than any previous generations living as young, unattached adults. There was a lot of speculation (and hope) that they would settle down when they married and face the responsibilities of parenthood. While they got married, they didn't settle down. Despite moving on in life, they still clung to their quintessential Boomer attitudes and values. They didn't automatically become their parents, as they continued to rewrite the rules or, more often than not, had the rules rewritten for them.

The generation that had won World War II had been, for the most part, frugal and willing to do without luxuries. The soldiers had learned how little they needed to survive when fighting at the front, and when they returned, they found it natural and acceptable to continue to suppress their own wants, needs and even opinions and ideas. At home, civilians had worked, scrimped and done without to do their part to help. For those of this older generation who had experienced the Great Depression, it was often hard to spend and even harder to borrow.

Born after these two formative events, the Boomers' orientation to sacrifice and personal indulgence was a product of their own time. Their attitudes toward spending and borrowing could not have been more different than their parents' attitudes. They were avid consumers who drew the line between necessities and luxuries at a very different spot on the scale from where their parents had.

In terms of economics, marriage didn't settle the Boomers down; it actually accelerated their buying behaviors. Most couples felt entitled to set up their own households right away rather than live with relatives while they built up a nest egg. The homes they started with were bigger than the homes their parents had started with, and were equipped with more modern amenities. Those who lived in the suburbs felt they needed a car and soon justified a second one. A television set (yes, that's what we called them) went from being a luxury to a necessity, and the number of them per household skyrocketed.

Becoming parents didn't slow the Boomers down either. When they had kids, they insisted on the best and latest equipment. They didn't want to give their children anything that they, themselves, would not accept as worthy. A new standard for quality was born.

How could they afford to do this? Counter-intuitively, all of their spending helped drive economic growth, which in turn drove job growth, and many jobs paid very good salaries. On top of this, whereas many of their parents may have benefited from the government's post-war GI programs, the Boomers often had a very different GI resource: Generous In-laws.

Boomers were distinct from earlier generations in yet another regard – they were more likely to have two-income families. This trend began when many Boomers began to feel, as a matter of principle, that both parents had a right to a career. It was simply incomprehensible to them that parenting responsibility might prevent them from achieving their full adult potential. For a generation that was accustomed to living on their its terms, this was another compromise that they simply weren't going to accept.

Dual incomes meant nearly twice as much spending, and the banking industry was committed to making spending easier. The Boomers' spending spree would be fueled by the expansion of credit. Any stigma once attached to owing money would soon disappear. And any stigma attached to borrowing was dwarfed by the Boomers' determination to have what they wanted, regardless of how they got it. Types of credit proliferated. The sheer size of credit ballooned.

The year 1966 would prove to be turning point in the widespread dissemination of general-purpose credit cards. Yes, there was indeed to be a future in plastics. Bank of America was first in franchising its BankAmericard to banks across the country, later evolving to become Visa. That same year, a group of banks got together and formed the InterBank Card Association, which led to the creation of MasterCard.

As the ease and availability of credit expanded Boomers' spending, they also began to develop a different attitude about what they bought, which led to different expectations. In their youth, marketing had taken a huge leap forward as logistical capabilities developed during the war made a more sophisticated distribution of goods possible. With broader distribution came increased competition and a wider spectrum of choice. Control continued to shift to the Boomer consumer.

Proliferation and competition created a new challenge for marketers. In many categories, growth would no longer come from simply increasing sales; now brands needed to do it at the expense of other brands by growing share of market. This was to be the beginning of the New Age of Marketing in which the discipline and art of branding were taken to new heights.

Today the term "branding" is nearly synonymous with the title of Brand Manager. The brand manager is responsible for designing and executing a marketing plan that grows the brand's reputation and its business. Since brands, and the people who manage them, were created in response to Boomers' unprecedented clout, we have coined them the Original Brand Managers. They were the original ones who fell in love with these brands and defined them. They felt as though they owned these brands (think Levi's) and, as such, they were the ones managing the requirements of what those brands needed to be.

Listerine was, for many years, the dominant brand in the mouthwash category. It had virtually created the home mouthwash category back in the 1920s when it was positioned as a cure for halitosis, a fancy word for bad breath. Listerine gave users a strong signal that it was working as it caused an unpleasant burning sensation in the mouth. It left one's breath smelling somewhat antiseptic and medicine-like, but that was seen as confirmation that it worked.

In response to the new preferences of Boomers, P&G launched Scope mouthwash in 1966. It tasted better, was less harsh in the mouth and left your breath feeling and smelling sweeter than Listerine. Scope also positioned itself in a way that repositioned the competition by referring to the Listerine benefit as "medicine breath." Scope was speaking Boomers' hedonistic language and its sales rocketed for years to come.

To get in front of consumer demand, companies started hiring more brand managers to design new brands in a way that created and maximized a company's portfolio of brands, many of which competed with each other in the same category for the same consumer. The discipline of brand marketing was evolving into the higher art of brand management.

Some marketers took this task more seriously than others, as I was to learn firsthand early in my advertising career. Fresh out of college, I started working at the Cunningham & Walsh advertising agency on Folgers Coffee, a brand then owned by P&G. At one point, I received a memo from the Folgers brand manager proposing countermeasures to defend against the introduction of a competitive coffee product from a new brand named Highpoint. As I girded my loins to wage battle against any competitor of my P&G client, and read on, to my great surprise, I learned that Highpoint was not a new entry from General Foods or Nestlé, but from P&G itself. Yikes. They were taking brand management seriously, and approaching it with military-like discipline and zeal.

One of our clients at Cunningham & Walsh was Scheiffelin & Somerset, importers of fine wines, champagne and distilled spirits. One of their most successful brands at the time was Blue Nun wine, the brainchild of Peter Sichel, the German-American wine merchant.

At the time, the typical American consumer had an extremely limited understanding of wine, and most were very intimidated when it came to choosing wine. While it's hard to believe by today's standards, if someone was going to drink wine, the hierarchy of choice was essentially red

GOLD
NUGGETS

Today, **63%** of Baby Boomer households
have **at least one person working full time**

In 2012, Baby Boomers accounted for **49%**
of all consumer packaged goods sales.

Contrary to popular conception, Baby Boomers
are **no more or less brand loyal** than their
younger counterparts.

U.S. adults **fifty and over** consume more than
forty hours of television per week.[6]

or white. Little attention was given to the wine's country of origin, and certainly less, if any, to the grape varietals with which it was made.

Sichel knew this, and he also knew that the complex name and nomenclature of his German Liebfraumilch wine would only add to their confusion. Brilliantly, and to the horror of his wine purist peers, he made his wine simpler by naming it in a simple way — Blue Nun. It went on to become the best-selling international wine in the world. Cunningham & Walsh personified the brand by creating a nun who wore a blue habit. We made the point that Blue Nun goes well with all foods by showing the Blue Nun going "anywhere and everywhere." Boomers loved it.

Years later, Boomers have made Yellow Tail wine a global success. Is there something to the power of color in a brand's success? Consider this.

When I was working at N.W. Ayer (America's first ad agency), I was assigned to the KitchenAid portable appliance business. Recently acquired from Hobart, they were located in a little schoolhouse in St. Joseph, Michigan, down the road and out of sight of Whirlpool's global headquarters. I'm not sure where the "s" on appliances came from, as KitchenAid had only the white stand mixer. In fact, we sold just as many dust covers for the mixer as we did mixers. When you were done using your mixer, you covered it to protect it and hide it.

In change there is opportunity, and we noticed that American homes were undergoing a significant structural change. Kitchens used to be functional work spaces in which the head of the household labored over the meal and then came through swinging doors to the dining room to present the meal to her family. In that environment, the appliances on your countertop were tools, and you took care of your tools by covering them to protect them from dust.

Now kitchens were being transformed from functional work spaces to the heart of the home. People were adding on to them, building "great rooms." Sofas, bookcases, TVs and, of course, telephones started appearing in kitchens. The kitchen island – the heart of the heart of the home – was becoming a "must-have" in fancier kitchens.

When kitchens became the heart of the home, the things on the countertop became home furnishings. And if they were going to be home furnishings, then style and design needed to become equal, if not greater than, function.

We brought this to life in advertising with a truly great theme line: KitchenAid: "For the Way It's Made." The line spoke to how well the product was made and how well the consumer could make great things, too.

That's when we said, "Why don't we make these things in colors other than white? If they're being used as home furnishings, shouldn't they come in different colors?" To make room for new colors on the manufacturing line, we discontinued the production of dust covers.

Without deliberately intending to, we had also solved one of KitchenAid's business problems. The KitchenAid stand mixer was, and still is, incredibly durable. It doesn't break down. Once consumers buy one, they can keep it forever.

By offering the stand mixer in a variety of new colors, we were creating the obsolescence that hadn't previously existed. The new colors were so irresistible that Boomers "needed" to have a new mixer even though their current one was built to work for another seventy years. Out with the old, in with the new. This was the beginning of the Boomers' new definition of "disposable" income.

The mixer color initiative went so well that we soon extended it to a full range of kitchen tools – toasters, blenders, food processors and coffee makers. In the end, we put the "s" in portable appliances.

A sage figure at my first agency defined advertising as the art of getting consumers to buy things they didn't know they needed. In the KitchenAid example, none of these Boomers needed a new mixer until a new need was created for them. It became absolutely necessary to own the latest home furnishing and culinary statement, just as the Boomers made it essential to own the latest and most stylish cars that Detroit knew they "needed."

During this early era of consumerism, Boomers grew up with the feeling that a new world was being built specifically for them. They were surrounded by a society that was profiting from making them happy, healthy and prosperous. Since this bred a sense of entitlement and empowerment that they never shed, as they reached adulthood and started families, the marketplace morphed itself around their sheer size and spending power. Indirectly, but unquestionably, their needs directed what everything from houses to soap looked like.

These were the years that Madison Avenue profited from the true meaning of this new generation: its magnitude. If marketers simply kept their sights focused on the eighteen to forty-nine target, the Boomers' population growth and expanding income alone would drive meaningful year-after-year growth. Add to this the increased sophistication in marketing and branding, combined with easy access to credit and, in short order, the Boomers had become the ultimate target audience in the history of marketing. If you worked on

Madison Avenue, the two martini lunch had just become the three martini lunch.

CHAPTER
FIVE

THE MOST VALUABLE
GENERATION™
Having the most and spending the most.

As Boomers moved along through their thirties, forties and fifties, they settled in at the top of the economic pyramid and reigned over an era of unprecedented prosperity. Their prosperity created a virtuous cycle – the more they spent, the more the economy grew, which meant they earned more and spent more. Paradoxically, they were their own growth engine. They were the Most Valuable Generation, a prime group of consumers living in their prime earning years.

When it came to owning things, their attitude was "money is no object." They were one of the most material generations ever, and their focus was shifting from owning something to owning something better or to owning more than one.

Boomers who already owned a nicer house than their parents did soon traded up to a better one and, in some cases, bought a second or third home. Boomers who had a reliable car bought a newer one (because Detroit made them "need" one) and often kept both cars. If they owned cars, why shouldn't their kids? Soon, many households, who a generation before did not own a single car, had three or four sitting in the driveway.

In investing, many Boomers felt that they had a Golden Touch, and why not? For most of their lives, their investments had grown and multiplied. In the late 1940s, the Dow Jones Industrial Average bounced along below the 200 mark. From the mid-1960s to the mid-1970s, it fluctuated and flirted with the 1,000 mark, and in the early 1980s it continued its steady ascent, closing above 10,000 before the year 2000 arrived.

While the Great Recession that began in 2008 has slowed the market's ascent, many expect to see it break through the 15,000 mark by the time this book hits the store shelves. Think of what this means – during the lifetimes of almost all Boomers, this widely respected economic indicator will have multiplied by at least fifteen times. During the lifetimes of some of the older Boomers, it has multiplied an astonishing seventy-five times.

The Boomers, by age and means, were living at the top of the economic pyramid and were enjoying their place in the sun. They believed that they had worked hard to earn this position in life and felt entitled to keep their possessions and positions. In a real-life version of their childhood game, they had become "King of the Mountain," and the view was pretty good.

Not everyone can be king. Some members of the newer generations have harbored animosity toward the Boomers, postulating that the Boomers had cornered the market on jobs, gamed the system and kept them out of the castle. Their accusations are not entirely untrue.

The Boomers continued to want what they wanted, and they tended to get what they wanted. They didn't see any reason why they should step aside from a hard-earned position in life simply to make room for a younger person. In true double-standard form, entitled Boomers began to look askance at Millennials and Gen X and Y, labeling them "entitled generations," job seekers who wanted to start at the top without "paying their dues." With more life experience and wisdom than the newer generations, the eternally young Boomers were not convinced that youth translated into better performance. The same workplace that once had a gender gap now had a generational gap. Bridging that gap would require finding common ground between two very different sets of generational values.

This values gap also fuels the passionate commentary about the future of Social Security. The younger generations have been suspiciously eycing Boomers for most of their lives and are gravely concerned that the Boomers' insistence on drawing a Social Security benefit ("We earned it, we're entitled to it, right?") and the sheer numbers in which they will do it will sink the system.

Regardless of what the real future of Social Security is, what's most relevant is the Boomers' indefatigable optimism about their financial future. On an irrational, emotional level, the Boomers do not believe that the well will ever run dry, and why should it? They are guided by their life experiences. While they have felt fluctuations and lived through setbacks, the predominant trend has always been prosperity. Prosperity had become popular and their generational, post-war bias is toward optimism. All this negative talk about Social Security simply sounds like countless other scares that never materialized. Nuclear annihilation? Never happened. Energy crisis? The tank is full. Retirement income? No problem.

To continue with the well analogy, the Boomers not only believe that the well will never run dry, they expect that it will actually continue to fill up. A recent Viagra ad aptly claims that older men are at an "age of knowing how to make things happen."

With respect to "the well," the Boomers are simultaneously optimistic that it will be full, and if by some chance it is not, they know they have the will and the means to somehow get more water. Rightfully or wrongfully, they are once again letting the experiences of their past guide their orientation toward the possibilities of the future.

The Boomers are going to go as far as they can with all that they've got for as long as they can. As they begin to age into their fifties and sixties, years in which previous generations retired, the Boomers won't be stopping. In fact, many will be just getting started. There is no intention to change, and no reason to even imagine that things might change.

While the Boomers were seeing no end in sight, the view from Madison Avenue was about to change dramatically. The Most Valuable Generation™, once the driving focus of growth, was soon to be seen from the rearview mirror.

CHAPTER
SIX

THE GRADUATING CLASS
*Aging out of marketing's eighteen
to forty-nine target.*

Without realizing it, the Boomers had become marketing's proverbial "boiled frog." The generation that thought it was ageless had actually gotten older, and in the process had aged out of marketing's fashionable eighteen to forty-nine target. This hadn't happened overnight – the Boomers had met their marketing fate the same way the frog did – from a gradual change in temperature that was imperceptible until its full effect was felt.

As I travel the speaking circuit, the question Boomers ask me most often is why they don't "get" many of today's ads. The answer is simple, but it is met with incredulity: "You don't get them because they weren't written for you." How could that be, they ask. Aren't we the ones who have loved these brands for all these years? How could they possibly write us out of the script when we still use their products? Bewilderment gives way to frustration and eventually anger. Eighty million of America's most valuable consumers are starting to realize that they've been scorned, and they aren't happy about it. Just as their sheer numbers had the ability to transform brands on the way up, their discontent can diminish these brands just as dramatically. They may have crossed the arbitrary line that has them aging out of marketing's sweet spot but they are no less valuable today than they were yesterday. They are to be ignored at one's peril.

Recently, I changed my pants.

Like many of my fellow Boomers, I've always worn Levi's and, as I like to say, I've been true blue. I've been fiercely loyal to Levi's because I see them as the quintessential original. My generation made them what they are, and as I've strived to be ageless, they have served as an indispensable link to my youth. They embody what I stand for and are inextricably linked with my hardworking, patriotic values. The thought of wearing another brand never crossed my mind until I saw a new Levi's advertising campaign that changed my mind, and my brand.

Far be it from a Boomer to know what today's typical twenty-something wants in a pair of jeans (I do know they've dropped the blue reference, though), but imagine my reaction when I saw a Levi's billboard displaying an off-putting, intertwined young couple that looked like an oversexed pair of jobless vagrants who didn't have enough money between them to buy a pair of jeans, let alone the two pairs of Levi's they were wearing.

I stood aghast at this portrayal of my beloved brand, wondering whose children these were, where they had gone wrong, and from whom they had stolen the money to buy their jeans (and tattoos). Right then and there, my lifelong values of hard work, honesty and dignity came into full conflict with Levi's portrayal of neo-idealism. If this startling image was meant to be a portrayal of what Levi's now believed its brand values were, then I had clearly missed the memo that something had changed. It was time for me to make a change too, and fast.

Sadly, I accepted the fact that Levi's no longer loved me and had jilted me in favor of a prospect allegedly more attractive than me. I went looking for love elsewhere.

After forty years of blind faith in Levi's, I discovered J.L. Powell, an Orvis-esque catalog retailer apparently conceived by Boomers for Boomers. Leafing through the catalog, I came across a great-looking pair of (blue) jeans, worn by an attractive, rugged guy my age. J.L. Powell was speaking my language. Now, here's a brand that understands me, I thought. I bought them immediately, and they have turned out to be a great pair of jeans.

Despite my love of the new J.L. Powell jeans, deep down I was still annoyed that Levi's went out of its way to make me switch brands. I was so annoyed, that I spoke to the new CEO of Levi Strauss & Co. Chip Bergh. It just so happens that Chip is a former client, longtime friend and one of the best marketers I have ever worked with. For all of you Boomer Levi's lovers out there, take solace in the fact that Chip is one of us, and he gets it. He has a deep understanding of the Levi's brand equity and I have no doubt that he will find a way to change things to continue to reward our lifetime of loyalty to this quintessentially great American brand.

For every Levi's story of Boomer and brand disconnect, there are a hundred more. Clearly, something had changed, but it wasn't the Boomers. Their numbers hadn't yet declined in any major way. They still had a dominant share of U.S. income and wealth and they were spending it as actively as ever. They were still the largest users of most all media and they continued to crave a strong relationship with the brands they loved most. They were still doing what they had always done during the go-go years of Madison Avenue. What could possibly have happened to cause this rift in the Boomer-brand relationships? Why would

GOLD
NUGGETS

Baby Boomers account for
1/3 of all Internet users,
including Facebook and Twitter users.

53% of all U.S. Baby Boomers are
Facebook users.

U.S. Adults fifty and over spend more
than **$7 billion per year** online.

In 2014, four in ten **wireless customers**
are Baby Boomers.[7]

any marketer allow this to happen? What line of thinking would lead a company to alienate so many of the very people who were in the best possible position to keep it growing?

The Boomers' priorities hadn't changed but Madison Avenue's had. The Boomers were aging out of the eighteen to forty-nine age bracket that had become the lucrative sweet spot that marketers directed their advertising to. Targeting the eighteen to forty-nine population had become a deeply ingrained best practice. All of the Industry's philosophies, process and tools had been optimized to appeal to this demographic, and it had become a definitive, seemingly irreversible part of the marketing mythology and culture for decades. Madison Avenue had profitably perfected the art of communicating to this age group and, as long as the party was still enjoyable, it was hard to leave.

The irony in shunning the age-fifty-and-over Boomers who have aged out of the lucrative eighteen to forty-nine cohort is that they were the ones that *created* it, beginning in 1964 when the first Boomer turned eighteen. An entire generation of marketers has been fishing in the bathtub – their task made easier by the presence of so many prospects in such a well-defined area.

For all of the reasons already discussed, the Boomers made many brands famous, and they also inspired enduring marketing practices. Marketers know that the fifty-and-over cohort is important, but they also believe that the eighteen to forty-nine consumers are the franchise of their future. In a world of limited resources, they are forced to choose one marketing target, and the inertia around eighteen to forty-nine makes it the default choice even though it's not always the right choice.

The other dynamic that perpetuates the popularity of the

eighteen to forty-nine target is Madison Avenue's infatuation with youth. It is hard to overstate how fundamental this is to the very being of the typical advertising agency.

Advertising has always been known as a young person's game. The industry has always believed that the ability to come up with fresh, new, award-winning creative ideas required the vigor, imagination and creativity that come with youth. Youth was said to provide freshness, the ability to be in sync with subtle movements in the zeitgeist, an edge that faded rapidly after just a few years in the business. Big agencies often had older people (aka grown-ups) in their management ranks, but when image mattered, they paraded their young geniuses in front of the creative world. Success required creativity, and creativity was presumed to be the province of youth.

It should come as no surprise then that the *average* age of an ad agency employee today is just twenty-nine. Think about that number. Not only is it just a few years older than college graduation age, but if it's the average age for an agency – many of which have a whole echelon of fifty-something "executives" – then they must have a pretty large contingent that's even *younger* than twenty-nine. Yikes. If I'm the client, I'm sure hoping that the presumption that youth leads to better ideas is correct.

My grandfather, a hardworking Yankee dairy farmer and proprietor of common sense, often said, "young people don't know what they don't know." Far be it from a farmer to be an expert on advertising, but I think what he was saying all those years ago was, "it takes one to know one."

The adoration of the eighteen to forty-nine cohort is perpetuated because the typical agency creative doesn't want to, and doesn't know how to, communicate to an older consumer. They don't want to because older people aren't cool, and if the target audience for your campaign is not cool, then there's little if no chance that you can do the cool work that will win you awards and get you a promotion. They don't know how to communicate to an older consumer because they've never been old themselves. They fundamentally lack the insight needed to "walk in the Indian's moccasins."

While no one was watching, most all of the Boomers have leaked out of the eighteen to forty-nine bucket and have been replaced by consumers who may never generate the per-capita value of The Most Valuable Generation™. The Boomers are too important to ignore. There is much to be gained by prioritizing them and much to be lost by taking them for granted. The Age of Aging has arrived, and the Boomers will demand a new marketing paradigm that ensures a new relationship with brands they want to love.

CHAPTER
SEVEN

STARTING OVER, AGAIN
So much for the simple life.

The story of the Boomers is a story of starts.

Our story began with the post-war peace and prosperity that *started* a baby boom and created a new generation that started an unprecedented transformation of culture, commerce and marketing. So far, our story has followed the Boomers from birth through adulthood. It has been a commentary on a pioneering generation that has been the first of its kind to do things the way they had never been done before. As they approach an age at which previous generations slowed down, the Boomers are showing no signs of relenting. In fact, a definitive chapter of their lives is about to draw to a close, but not surprisingly, they are already writing the script for another new beginning.

The Western view of life has always focused on a beginning and an end. Previous generations embraced this notion, with most working a lifetime in a single career with a single employer in exchange for the promise of a comfortable retirement. Their work ethic was prolific because the years spent working were finite and gave way to a predictable period of extended rest. The path was clear and linear: life started and ended, and you made the most out of what you had along the way.

As we have referenced, this way of life evolved not because the subsequent generation willed a change, but because circumstances had changed. Our expanding economy and prosperity were creating choice and opportunity. With this came flexibility and options for workers that created a new attitude toward employment. The way in which one lived the middle of his or her life was changing for the better.

As this was happening, the workers' children were coming of age and developing a new set of values that they would bring to the workplace. By the time the Boomers were ready to work, the employer/employee contract was ripe for real change – the beginnings of a "free-agency" labor force were under way.

The Boomers brought their optimism and will to a job market that was malleable. The sheer numbers of like-minded Boomers in the workplace made Boomer-responsive change inevitable. As loyalty diminished, so too did the one-career/one-employer model. The Boomers were now experimenting with different job fields and different employers, which meant that they were starting and restarting their careers several times over. Eventually, the notion of life having just a beginning and an end didn't seem to make much sense with so many restarts in the middle. The "simple life" was over.

I have spent most of my life fishing with a core group of friends. With each year, the group gets smaller and our bucket list of places to fish gets longer. As we plan our annual trips, we inevitably bump up against the demands of life. There's always an excuse why one or more of us can't go, and with our attitude of "all of us or none of us," it has made for some pretty intense negotiating over the years. This went on for some time until we came up with a simple solution, and now we all peacefully drop everything when it's time to go fishing. The solution? We simply ask each other, "How long are you going to be dead for?" Like most Boomers, we're going to pack as much into this lifetime as we can, regardless of what it takes. If the previous generation lived "the simple life," we're determined to live "the full life" with a vengeance.

The unwritten rule of the full life is to stay in motion by constantly restarting. This sounds simple enough except for the fact that there is an enormous stop sign looming in the Boomers' future – they are reaching the end of their peak years of traditional employment. For some years, the average Boomer's daily lifestyle has been defined by his or her work. They have been waking up at home, commuting to work and returning home at the end of the day, only to start the routine all over again the next day. With work being one of their primary life-requirements, it has been consuming the majority of their life energy and dramatically shaping their lifestyle.

Now imagine what happens when this über-influential activity goes away. You can stop imagining because the largest generation in history is starting to exit the traditional workplace at the eye-popping rate of 10,000 a day, a trend that will continue every day for the next seventeen years.[8] Since we know they're not going to stop, the operative questions now are what will they do next? and where will they do it?

Many Boomers will need to continue to work as a matter of economic necessity. Close to two-thirds of Boomers aged fifty to sixty-four lost money during the Great Recession, with 20% of them losing up to 40% of their retirement savings. This and other considerations (e.g., fewer pension benefits) have a full 60% of them postponing plans for retirement.[9]

By virtue of their numbers, those that stay in or return to the traditional workplace will create an aging workforce the likes of which has never been seen before. This new fifty-five and over workforce will grow more rapidly than ever before, representing an unprecedented 18.7% of the labor force, and close to 93% of the expected growth in the U.S. labor force over the next three years.

Many of these Boomers plan on working past the age of sixty-five owing to a significant differential in Social Security benefits. An average worker retiring today at age sixty-two would receive a $2,639.00 a month benefit, versus $4,675.00 if they waited to age seventy-two, a compelling 75% increase in income.[10]

Many will take personal responsibility for their employment. This will give way to one of the most pronounced periods of entrepreneurialism and small business creation that our country has ever seen. Estimates indicate that there are currently five million Boomer entrepreneurs in the U.S., a figure that is expected to grow.[11] We are already seeing an astounding amount of energy and passion being brought to new enterprises, most for profit but many for non-profit as well.

While many Boomers will be focused on sustaining their income, many others will have the means to shift their focus from the workplace to home. These Boomers are coming home and they're committed to staying home and as 78% of adults between the ages of fifty and sixty-four have indicated a preference to age in place at a time when one-third of American households are home to one or more residents sixty years of age or older.[12]

As the eight or more hours a day that were spent at work are reallocated to the home, the dynamic of how the home will be used and how lives are lived within it will undergo sweeping change. Home-centric patterns of living will give rise to a series of changes that will have significant impact on the consideration, choice and use of an endless array of products and services. Home-centricity is a potent trend within the larger aging trend.

As they spend more time at home, these Boomers will spend time and money on things they value – for example, remodeling, home entertainment, cooking and collecting, as well as the things they missed out on while working, such as do-it-yourself handiwork, gardening and fun-time with children and grandchildren. ("Isn't it time we put that pool in?") Paradoxically, the more time they spend at home, the more they will want to get away from home, so we can expect them to spend more time dining out, shopping, traveling and getting together with friends.

Whether they are continuing to work or are enjoying some hard-earned time off, most Boomers did not adequately save for their future during their prime earning years. Their failure to do so can be attributed to this generation's bias toward a mix of hedonism and optimism. Throughout their lives they have lived in the moment, spending hard-earned money on short-term pleasure. While they intrinsically knew that a longer-term savings strategy was the prudent course, their optimistic view of life trumped all considerations. The Boomer attitude has always been, "I'll figure it out when the time comes because I always have and always will."

While many Boomers will reinvent themselves for commercial gain, others will look to reorient themselves to fulfill a new life agenda. The accumulated experience of a lifetime combined with the urgency brought on by aging will compel many to do things they have aspired to do for years. Interestingly, Boomers have been one of the fastest-growing demographics at U.S. divinity schools, according to the Association of Theological Schools (ATS), an organization of more than 250 theological graduate schools in the U.S. and Canada. The under-thirty crowd may still be the largest cohort of students – accounting for a third of the total – but the fifty-or-older group grew from

12% of students in 1995 to 20% in 2009, the most recent year for which data is available.[13]

Others are brimming with knowledge, confidence and curiosity and are determined to experiment and discover. These are the Boomers that Jane Pauley spoke of in the Foreword – countless folks who are re-imagining life in the later years of their lives. They are seeking joy and doing incredible things that even they themselves would not have believed possible years before. The ability and courage to re-imagine is truly a capability that comes with maturity.

This completes the story of the life of the Boomers. The goal has been to bring meaning to the generation that once searched for the meaning of life because meaning brings us understanding. The most effective marketing is that which reflects a truly deep understanding of the consumers it targets. That deep understanding requires a penetrating assessment of the consumer, not only at a point in time but over time. Said simply, the Boomers will defy understanding unless you get in touch with their values that were formed many years ago in a bygone context.

The value in marketing to Boomers is staggering, and to succeed, you must dig deeply to unearth the values that influence their behavior. The analogy to mining for gold is clear and compelling. The miners of '49 shared the same motivation as today's marketers – quick success – and their tactics (albeit primitive) were remarkably similar.

PART
TWO

LESSONS FROM THE
FIRST GOLD RUSH

CHAPTER
EIGHT

EUREKA!
Getting excited to get rich.

The Old Rush offers extraordinary value for marketers, in part because it is virgin territory.

Few things are more motivating than the prospect of getting rich, quickly. When word of the discovery of gold in California first spread, it was the true opportunists who responded first. To use our modern parlance, these were the original "first movers," people with entrepreneurial instincts who literally moved west as fast as they could to be the first ones on the gold. Many struck it rich by striking first, and it is this opportunistic interpretation of the Gold Rush that has it continuing to be an apt metaphor for entrepreneurialism even to this day.

If you're a marketer and if I've told the story well enough so far, you should be raring to join what I call "The Old Rush" – a modern-day chance to "strike it rich" by prioritizing the highly valuable, aging consumer. To do so, you must be every bit as opportunistic as the miners were, and you must move quickly to secure the riches first. While there is no learning precedent for marketing to the Baby Boomer Generation in their fifties, we do have the Gold Rush, and the analogies are remarkably relevant.

You probably already know a little bit about the California Gold Rush of the mid-nineteenth century. It began in 1848 when James W. Marshall – a carpenter and sawmill operator – found gold at Sutter's Mill in Coloma, California. Word of the discovery spread quickly, and by the end of the following year, some 300,000-plus prospectors (aka '49ers) had endured tremendous hardship to travel to California, not just from the United States, but from virtually every region of the world.[1] Many recall the Gold Rush as a domestic phenomenon, and similarly, many see the aging of Boomers as a uniquely American development. In truth, aging and the concept of The Old Rush is every bit as global as the original Gold Rush, but infinitely more valuable.

By the time the Gold Rush was over, gold worth tens of billions in today's dollars had been discovered.[2] Many had succeeded, and just as many had returned empty-handed, but the lore of this mania would prove to be universal and lasting.

To help you get a sense of what it was like to be a '49er, I'd like to introduce you to one of them: Alfred T. Jackson. Jackson kept a diary from May 19, 1850, to June 13, 1852. His diary was transcribed and published with commentary by C. L. Canfield in 1906. In his diary, Jackson describes his trials and tribulations in mining for gold in Rock Creek, California, during these same years.[3]

From Jackson's experiences, we will highlight three implications that are relevant to The Old Rush: the importance of being opportunistic, the need to be resourceful and the commitment to persevere over adversity.

Like most, he started off with the notion that he would make his fortune quickly and then return home to settle back into a normal life. A true optimist, Jackson had it all planned out.

He would get rich quickly and return to the town of Norfolk, Connecticut, to marry his sweetheart, Hetty North, and get on with real life.

Jackson's diary starts as he is starting his quest for gold. He has sacrificed everything to make the trip and has almost nothing to his name. He is eking out a meager existence next to a small creek in the desolate hills:

"May 19, 1850: The pork I bought in town last night is the stinkiest salt junk ever brought around the Horn. It's a hardship that we can't get better hog meat, as it's more than half of our living. We fry it for breakfast and supper, boil it with our beans, and sop our bread in the grease."

Despite these conditions, Jackson was actually eating better than a lot of the other miners nearby, simply because he was more resourceful. He proudly notes that, "the boys all say that I am the best bread baker on the creek." In addition to baking, he also hunted for fresh food. In his second entry he reports:

"May 26, 1850: Went hunting this morning; killed seventeen quail and four pigeons. They make a good stew if the rotten pork didn't spoil it, but it's better than the bull beef the butcher packs around."

Success in the Gold Rush was all about the survival of the fittest, the most primal version of perseverance. Jackson arrived fit and able, and adapted well to his new conditions. Optimism was the best antidote to omnipresent hardship:

"July 7, 1850: If I can save enough to buy the Slocum farm next to our place and Hetty says 'yes', I'll have that "little house and little wife" and that will be about all I want on this earth. I would like to have enough capital so that I would not have to slave from sunrise till dark as I did on dad's farm. I don't know as the work was any harder than what we do here, but there is a difference. There all we got was just about a bare living, at the best, a few hundred dollars put away for a

year's work, but here one doesn't know what the next stroke of the pick, or the next rocker full of dirt, may bring forth... That is the excitement and fascination that makes one endure the hardships."

Later in the diary, he is more explicit about how excited he and his fellow '49ers were about the prospect of getting rich:

"November 24, 1850: When I think of how much money I am making it seems like a dream. I used to work for a dollar a day during haying time... The regular miners' wages here are eight dollars a day and very few men will hire out."

While it clearly required resourcefulness, perseverance and optimism to succeed once you got to the Gold Rush, imagine what it took to make the decision to go there in the first place. Choosing to go to the Gold Rush posed significant financial risk and real physical danger for a reward that was both mysterious and elusive. Yet hundreds of thousands looked the other way on this risk. Why would otherwise rational people who were leading good lives take on this excessive risk? They were seduced by the mysterious power of *mania*.

Inherent in the word "rush" is a strong element of mania. Mania was the phenomenon that lured countless conservative folks to risk all for a chance at gold, and it is best defined as an addictive and excessive level of unreasonable enthusiasm.

With every year that I spend in advertising, I develop a deeper and more perplexing awe of how "unreasonable" normally reasonable people can be. By "unreasonable" I don't mean stubborn or disagreeable; instead, I mean to suggest that they make important decisions with little or no rational reason, thought or assessment.

Think about the thought process that goes into buying most people's two biggest assets: their house and their automobile.

While the purchase process always begins with well-thought-out intent, a budget and a plan, in the end, the decision is often driven by some instinctual, irrational motivation that triumphs over reason. Whether it's the dream house that you can't live without or the new Ford F250 with more torque than you need, in the end it's not reason that leads to action, it's emotion.

Similarly, the decision to join the Gold Rush was fundamentally unreasonable. True, but just how unreasonable was it when many other "normal" people were making the same choice, with the same excessive, unreasonable enthusiasm that seems aberrant at first but is then sanctioned and perpetuated by the participation of others? Mania is the ground zero of most all trends, fads and viral outcomes.

The Old Rush is the next mania. The prospect of quick success in targeting the aging consumer is exciting, but excitement alone is insufficient – recall that there were many excited prospectors who never got on the road to California as well as those that did get on the road but never got there.

The miners that made it had a serious case of gold fever. They didn't just idly dream about the opportunity, they believed in it with every fiber of their being. They had a vision, a plan and the dedication and strength to persevere over adversity. They willed success.

That which fueled these opportunists should fuel you. As has always been true of trendsetters, those who identify and act on the opportunity first will be judged and questioned by conventional minds. However, all conservatism is abandoned once the precedent of success is established. Someone in your product category or market is going to join The Old Rush first, and if they execute properly, they will be successful.

Once the success of the first movers is made known, true

GOLD NUGGETS

LEVI STRAUSS & COMPANY – FROM GOLD RUSH OUTFITTER TO AMERICAN ICON

In addition to creating a state (California was a Mexican territory when gold was discovered) *and* prompting the building of a great deal of transcontinental infrastructure, the Gold Rush gave birth to many new business ventures, some of which are still thriving today. The enterprise perhaps most associated with the California Gold Rush is **Levi Strauss & Company**.

The company was founded in 1853 when Levi Strauss, who was born in Bavaria and immigrated with his family to the U.S., moved from New York to San Francisco to open up a new branch of his family's dry goods business. Strauss had a great deal of canvas in inventory because he was expecting to sell a lot of tents to miners and prospectors. Instead what he discovered was very little demand for tents but a great unmet need for durable work pants. He quickly started making and selling canvas pants that could stand up to the tough work of mining and prospecting, even if they weren't exactly that comfortable. Twenty years later, Strauss switched to a more pliable, blue denim fabric and created the first of the blue jeans so beloved by Baby Boomers.[4]

Levi Strauss & Company continues to leverage its Gold Rush heritage to this day as the Name Sponsor of the new home of the NFL's San Francisco 49ers.

mania ensues. By the time the trend followers catch up with the trendsetters, most of the easy pickings will be gone. By analogy, the early '49ers found nuggets on the ground – those who came later had to work much harder, breaking ground and digging deep to find smaller gold worth less.

In every marketplace, there are leaders and followers, and each group succeeds in its own way. The Old Rush demands leaders.

To motivate your organization, you will have to overcome the inertia of convention – that is, the built-up bias that says that marketing to youth is the future of the franchise. Change is hard, but so again is fast growth. The '49ers were leaders and risk takers, and while there never was (and never is) a guarantee of success, they at least positioned themselves to succeed by moving to where the gold was. The Old Rush is here, and it's time to get moving.

CHAPTER
NINE

DESTINATION GOLD
Leaving familiarity behind.

**To succeed in the Old Rush, you will need
to abandon some supposedly
"tried and true" ideas.**

In the mid-nineteenth century, the notion of Manifest
Destiny – the idea that it was the United States' destiny
to expand from its foothold in the eastern part of North
America until it went from "sea to shining sea" – had a
lot to do with our country's western orientation. Although it
was primarily driven by a spirit of nationalism and obligation,
Manifest Destiny presented itself in largely economic
ways. Westward expansion was to be a boon for American
entrepreneurs, and the Gold Rush was its accelerant.

Multinational marketers seeking fast growth in today's global
economy are constantly looking for the next white-space –
geographical market spaces that are still underdeveloped
and are ripe for rapid growth. One can only imagine how
enticing westward expansion must have been to American
industrialists in the late 1800s.

Expanding west, whether to establish territory or seek
gold, required leaving the East. Just as the West became
synonymous with opportunity, we will use the East to signify

the status quo, or the place or state of mind one had to depart from to get somewhere else.

No other topic in business is as published as leadership. While this is meant to be a book on the opportunities inherent in aging, it also speaks to the power of leadership. Those who will gain the most in The Old Rush, like those before them in the Gold Rush, will be those who literally lead by acting first. The aspects of leadership that will be most relevant are the need for a clear vision, to take initiative and to make tough choices.

For those leaders who led the way to the Gold Rush, the vision was brutally clear. Gold had been discovered, it was extremely valuable, and those that found it first would find the most. The irrationality around the mania of the Gold Rush probably blurred this vision somewhat, but despite the haze, the sight was still pretty clear. Smart people were going to make a lot of money.

Whereas much has been written about the character of the '49ers once they were *on* the gold, much less attention has been given to the character of the men that compelled them to go *to* the gold. Were the original '49ers greedier than the following waves of prospectors? Surely, there was plenty of greed to go around, but greed alone was probably insufficient when it came to the hard choice of going for gold. These were leaders who had a vision and knew how to exercise initiative.

Initiative is fundamentally about action. A vision without initiative is nothing more than a dream. As the Gold Rush unfolded, the dreamers stayed home and the leaders with initiative acted and moved westward where they would be rewarded for their pioneering spirit. In choosing to move, they fundamentally had to leave something behind: their East.

Take our miner friend Alfred Jackson, whom we introduced in the last chapter. When news of gold first arrived, Jackson was enjoying the same lifestyle as many other rural New Englanders of the time. He was working the land and sustaining himself reasonably comfortably. In considering the Gold Rush, Jackson was not escaping the squalor of an urban slum or fleeing the law or a broken life – no, things were good for him. Instead, his decision to join the Gold Rush was driven by a desire to improve his lot in life. In fact, he had a pretty practical plan – he intended to go west, strike it rich quickly and return home just as fast. Using today's vernacular, Jackson was a leader who had a plan to take him from good to great.

For the vast majority of leaders like Jackson who achieved their version of greatness in the gold fields, they needed to leave something behind. The metaphorical East that these pioneers would leave behind consisted of many things – such as homes, farms, family, loved ones and sustainable lifestyles. While the things that represented the status quo were different for everyone, there was one common theme: the courageous leaders who would take the initiative to head west and prospect for great wealth were willing to leave *familiarity* behind. More on that later.

So off they went – fearless leaders who had a vision and were intent on achieving their dreams at any cost. Once there, they staked the most productive claims quickly and racked up some early wins. As anticipated, more and more prospectors were arriving every day, and their numbers seemed to be expanding exponentially.

Note Jackson's diary entries:

"March 30, 1851: It is astonishing how many people are coming to California. The hills are crowded with miners and prospectors."

Not only had Jackson arrived early, but he had done so at a time when a single person had a reasonable chance of finding gold. Those who came after him not only had to work harder, they had to work in teams. The cost of doing business had just skyrocketed:

> *"April 25, 1852: I notice that the miners now, instead of mining alone, or with a single partner, as was generally the rule at first, have got to forming companies of a half a dozen or a dozen men and working their claims more systematically and extensively. Ounce diggings are not as easily found as they were a year or two ago and the creeks, gulches and shallow places are pretty well worked out."*

Under these circumstances, our early leaders now needed to adapt – they needed to innovate to maintain their first-mover advantage. They needed an eagerness to try new things, to continue to take new risks. Once a labor-intensive endeavor, prospecting was becoming a mechanized and capital-intensive industry. While competition was increasing, our leaders would again be rewarded for their initiative as they were able to reinvest their sizable initial gains in their own mechanization (applied to the most productive, early claims) to keep yields high and maintain the lead versus the newcomers.

If you aspire to meet with similar success in The Old Rush, you will need a special breed of leadership defined by vision, initiative and decisiveness. While this book will go on to offer advice on many aspects of leadership in marketing, the primary lesson to be gleaned from this chapter on the Gold Rush is the importance of understanding your "East" and being willing to leave it behind to win in your "West."

If we define the West as marketing to the lucrative white-space that is the fifty-plus Baby Boomers, then the East must be today's common practice of marketing to the eighteen to forty-nine cohort. Prioritizing the eighteen to forty-nine demographic has led to great success for many, not because the age range of eighteen to forty-nine has some magical quality to it, but because the eighteen to forty-nine cohort was populated by the largest generation in the history of marketing throughout the lifetime of many of today's marketers and top brands. If marketing to the eighteen to forty-nine cohort usually met with success, then it was understandable for there also to be a certain amount of comfort associated with that target choice – comfort derived from *familiarity*.

Marketers who want to capture the fast-growth potential in The Old Rush will fundamentally need to leave familiarity behind. This is a choice that conflicts with one of the core tenets of most corporate marketing cultures – best practices.

Holding marketers to a standard of best practices is praised because it grounds an organization's marketing in its historical successes. By replicating what has been done before, the likelihood of success is greater because the likelihood of risk is lower. In other words, what's familiar works.

Yes, most if not all of the current best practices are based on past successes achieved with marketing to the eighteen to forty-nine cohort. Continuing to use these best practices, however, erroneously assumes that the complexion and character of the eighteen to forty-nine group has not changed. Pardon the pun, but the target has moved.

Obviously, it's time to start creating some new best practices for the over-fifty consumer. The first step in moving ahead is to leave some of the misconceptions about marketing and aging behind.

You will need to *stop* believing that:
• Age is a number.
• Older consumers are less valuable than younger ones.

GOLD NUGGETS

NORDSTROM'S DEPARTMENT STORES – FROM GOLD TO SHOES AND MORE

The **Nordstrom Department Store** empire has its roots in the Klondike Gold Rush, about fifty years after the one in California. In search of opportunity, John W. Nordstrom immigrated to the United States from northern Sweden in 1887. He ended up in the northwest and tried his hand at potato farming near Seattle, and then in 1897 he joined the hearty adventurers who traveled north to the forbidding Yukon Territory where gold had been discovered.

Nordstrom put in two hard years before he made a modest gold strike. Even though his claim was disputed, he was ultimately able to sell it for about $13,000 – a considerable fortune at the time. Rather than stay in the Yukon Territory to look for more gold, Nordstrom took his newfound wealth and moved to Seattle, where he married Hilda Carlson and co-founded a shoe store.

To this day, Nordstrom's – now a national chain of upscale, fashion-forward department stores – is still known for its shoe departments and for its high level of customer service. The company is closely held and still led by a descendant of John W. Nordstrom.[5]

- It's better to build a franchise on a foundation of youth.
- Old is not fashionable.

You will need to *start* believing that:
- Aging is the future of living.
- Older consumers have the money. It takes money to increase sales.
- Brand franchises are built on loyalty, not age.
- Fashion is in the eye of the beholder.

While leaving familiarity behind feels risky, don't lose too much sleep over it. The core principles of marketing to eighteen to forty-nine are infinitely transferable to a fifty-plus model. *What* you need to do to create brand preference, and loyalty with an older consumer won't change a whole lot. The key difference – and the learning curve – will be in the *how*. Did any of the '49ers know *how* to prospect for gold before they headed west? Not a one. Yet they were not deterred by that which they *did not* know because they were willing to rely on what they *did* know. They looked for the answers within themselves and realized that they were smart, resourceful and determined enough to figure it out.

When I left my job at a large, successful advertising agency to start BoomAgers, I left the familiar behind. Never before had I started my own company, and never had so much been at stake. What I lacked in experience I made up for with will. When I look back on my leap of faith, the chasm doesn't look nearly as deep. If I knew then what I know now, I would not have looked down, I would have only looked forward.

CHAPTER
═══ TEN ═══

GEARING UP
What you need to succeed.

To succeed in The Old Rush, you will not only need to leave some things behind, you will also need to acquire some new strategies and tools.

Pursuing a high-stakes, high-risk endeavor like the Gold Rush required the utmost in planning. We've learned that the most successful miners had many of the hallmarks of strong leaders, but they were also meticulous planners. The logistics of traveling west to the gold fields were daunting enough, but once there, the miners also needed to acquire claims, mining know-how and essential gear. Under ordinary circumstances, this would have been an extraordinary undertaking, but there was nothing normal about the Gold Rush. Much, if not all, of what these courageous entrepreneurs were doing, they were doing for the first time ever, with no known precedent.

The planning requirements for the Gold Rush essentially fell into two categories: what you needed in order to get *to* the gold, and what you needed to *get* the gold.

The first thing one needed to get to the gold was a ride. The least appreciated aspect of the Gold Rush was the ordeal that most of the miners went through just to travel to California.

Infrastructure that we take for granted today simply did not exist. There were no continuous roads or railroads to the West, which meant that a miner needed to either travel by boat or patch together a cross-country excursion, both of which were lengthy, perilous and expensive.

For an East Coast prospector, there were essentially three options for getting to California, two by sea and one by land. By sea, one could travel by boat via Panama or Cape Horn. By land, one could take the California Trail, a time-consuming, two-thousand-mile trek via rail, wagon, horse and foot.

Another breed of prospector was the immigrant. Let's not forget that the Gold Rush was a global phenomenon. Thousands came from every corner of the globe, helping to swell San Francisco's population from about 800 in 1848 to over 50,000 in 1849.[6] One of the greatest migrations and immigrations in American history was under way.

When word of gold first got out, there were virtually no boat options for prospectors of average means; sufficient and affordable supply had not yet been established to meet the great new demand. However, those who were wealthy enough to own their own boats got to the gold first and soon added to their existing good fortune. Money begot money.

In a fortuitous twist of fate, a good number of the early contingents to sail to the gold fields were whaling families from Nantucket. For the better part of the first half of the nineteenth century, Nantucket was the whaling capital of the world, launching vessels and crews that traveled to the far reaches of the Pacific in search of whales. At the time, whale oil was the primary source of illumination and it fetched enormous prices on the world's markets. The Nantucket whalers were exceptional seamen and no strangers to danger. They took great risk, but they were generously rewarded for their successes. Whaling was a mania not all that different from the Gold Rush.

Toward the middle of that century, circumstances began to conspire against the wealthy Nantucket whaling families. Having depleted the stock of nearby Atlantic whales, Nantucketers were now traveling around Cape Horn to the Pacific, taking on more expense and risk for the same return. At the same time, the busy Nantucket harbor was silting in, which prevented the largest vessels from efficiently off-loading their cargo. Nearby New Bedford quickly seized on the opportunity, and diverted lucrative business away from Nantucket.[7]

However, the straw that really broke the whaling industry's back was the discovery of petroleum in Pennsylvania in 1849. Just as one door closed, another opened, and no one was better suited to capitalize on the bounty of the Gold Rush than the industrious, boat-owning Nantucket whaling families. Their trip to California was faster and easier than most, and their eventual Gold Rush success was so significant that many of them became and remain household names to this day, notably the Macy and Folger families.

It did not take long for two conventional boat routes to be established in 1849, marking the beginning of a ten-year migration to California.

The trips typically began on the Atlantic Coast and involved one of two routes either via Cape Horn or via Panama.

The Panama route was the quickest of the two but also presented the greatest risk. Boats would steam down to the Panama Isthmus, where passengers would disembark and begin an arduous journey through the jungles of Panama, to be met by a San Francisco–bound steamer on the west coast of the Isthmus. Many never finished the connection. Disabling and deadly blunts of malaria and cholera were all too common and claimed many before they could stake a claim for gold.

The alternative route was longer and only modestly safer. This trip involved sailing all the way south to round Cape Horn, proceeding north to San Francisco on the same boat. Think six months of sea sickness, poor food and water, and monotony.

Traveling by land was no less of an ordeal and was a nine-month undertaking that required extensive preparation. Although all of the land travelers experienced hardship, those who had prepared properly persevered, whereas those less organized either turned back or perished after they ran out of supplies and money. The road to richness turned to poverty and peril for the ill prepared.

Once the fortunate prospectors got to California, the next stage of critical planning kicked in: amassing the tools needed to mine for gold and the provisions necessary to survive in the wilderness for extended periods of time. This gearing-up process had all of the hallmarks of modern day supply chain management.

Our friend Jackson had to gear up, but he also had to identify the optimal amount of supplies to help him travel light in search of a claim while also having enough food to stay on the claim if it proved prosperous.

His simple provisions served him well, but as he became more ambitious and took on a partner (aka Pard), he needed to scale up his operation and provision accordingly:

"December 22, 1850: I've been to Sacramento...

*I bought a mustang and saddle, paid sixty dollars for the
horse and seventy-five for the saddle and bridle."*

As is so often the case, scaling his business (adding a horse)
meant adding complexity. He needed to feed the horse:

*"December 29, 1850: Green feed is plenty, but no oats or grain to
be had for love or money. We had to get some feed in case of snow, so
Christmas day I rode to Centerville and found a man who had cut some
wild oats in a valley below that town. He wanted two hundred and
fifty dollars a ton and fifty dollars more for delivering it on Rock Creek,
and I bought it at that figure."*

Jackson had no choice but to find more affordable fodder for
the horse, so he geared up again, but differently:

*"June 15, 1851: We have kept the horse...and there is plenty
of feed for him now. The hills are covered with grass, but later
in the year it all burns up and then we have to provide fodder.
There is a clearing up on the mountain of some dozen acres where
the grass grew pretty rank and we concluded we would cut
and stack it for winter use. I had a dickens of a time finding a scythe
and a rake. And had to ride down a valley below Rough and Ready
before I could get them. The owner would not sell, but agreed to loan
them for a week provided I would pay ten dollars for their use."*

Whether it was about getting to The gold or getting the gold
out of the ground, planning was an absolutely critical skill.
It often was the deciding factor between success and failure,
which in the gold fields ran the extremes of wealth and death.

Compared to the Gold Rush, gearing up for The
Old Rush is relatively simple but no less critical to
success. You will need two plans: one to seize the
initiative and get moving, and another to determine
strategy once "there." In executing both, you will need to

GOLD NUGGETS

MORE CALIFORNIA GOLD RUSH NUGGETS

Several other great American industrialists got their start during the Gold Rush, including:

- **Philip Armour**, who would found a meatpacking business in Chicago that grew into a global empire, made his fortune operating the sluices that controlled the flow of water into the rivers being mined.

- **John Studebaker** manufactured wheelbarrows for Gold Rush miners and went on to build one of America's great automobile fortunes.

- Two enterprising businessmen named **Henry Wells** and **William Fargo** moved to open an office in San Francisco, where they provided banking and shipping services to miners. Their company soon grew to become one of America's best-known financial institutions.[8]

be as agile as the '49ers were in adapting to changing circumstances.

As a marketer reading this book for the first time, you are no different from an entrepreneur who has just learned that gold was discovered at Sutter's Mill. There's a good chance you've never tried to mine the fifty-plus audience, and if so, you probably don't have a plan either. What you do have is wherewithal and resources, and, as with the '49ers, that's all it takes to get started.

As you start to plan, remember that most of the "easy gold" was gone as early as mid-1849. It is critical that your Old Rush start-up plan make initiative and speed to market paramount. Further, there will likely be gaps in your knowledge and, if so, planning for the unknown will be difficult if not impossible. Work quickly to determine what you and your organization need to know about the fifty-plus consumer, your brand and your category, and develop a "plan within the plan" to gain intelligence and insight.

Once done, you will end up with a rough map pinpointing your general destination and some options for getting there.

Provisioning comes next. What types of people, partners and resources will you need to execute your plan for getting to The Old Rush? The route you take to get there will determine what you need to take with you. Keep it simple and don't "over pack." You can't afford to have a cumbersome process slow you down as you are trying to speed your way to unexplored, virgin territory.

The overriding message here is if you want to get rich in The Old Rush, you will need to act quickly but plan carefully. History tells us that speed was of the essence in the Gold Rush, and if so, we would be smart to heed that precedent.

At the same time, speed was the undoing of many aspiring prospectors who acted so quickly that they planned poorly.

As with most business choices, balance is the key. You and your organization will need to determine how much rush is necessary to capitalize on The Old Rush. Act too quickly and you may risk executing ineffectively. Act too slowly, and the best plan in the world may not make up for the missed opportunity. Most of the '49ers didn't overthink this. There was simply too much at stake so they started heading west and fine-tuned their plan along the way.

CHAPTER
ELEVEN

STAKING A CLAIM
Knowing where the gold is.

**In The Old Rush, your chances of success will
reflect how well you have defined your target.**

U p to this point, we have been following the journey
of entrepreneurs who had a dream of gold. When
they arrived safely in California, they became
prospectors, gearing up to stake a claim for a
chance to become a miner.

As the gear-laden miners left the growing cities for the mining
fields, they needed to know where to look for gold. Once they
found a promising site, they also needed some assurance as
to its productivity before staking a claim and committing
resources to a fixed location.

Jackson, our diary-keeping '49er, spent a lot of time
thinking about the patterns in which gold was found. As he
prospected the countryside for the ideal claim, he watched
to find out which other claims were paying off. He listened
to learn how rich those claims were and at what depth
the gold started, how deep it went and whether it
extended horizontally. Jackson was smart. He was ready to
work hard. But he wanted to be sure that he was working

a claim that had the best chance of yielding a fortune. He was also eager to partner up with someone he trusted, not only to protect his claim, but to work it harder for a greater yield, faster.

Gold's distinct properties made mining during the Gold Rush possible but also extremely frustrating. Much of the California gold lay buried under thick layers of dirt in seemingly random areas. Some of it was under streambeds, but much of it was buried high up in the hills.

In the absence of geological maps and technology, how did a prospector decide where to dig? Not surprisingly, one of the best strategies was to dig where gold had already been found. This was easier said than done, as successful miners tended to be secretive and sought to keep their claims to themselves. Jackson was lucky – when his first claim petered out, a friend on the creek let him in on a rich claim in exchange for help digging a ditch to divert some of the creek:

"July 21, 1850: Anderson offers me a share in his claim.
He's working a dry gulch just about a half a mile north of the
cabin. It's rich on the bed-rock, but he has to strip down about ten feet
of top dirt, and then pack the gravel down to the creek
a couple of hundred yards."

When that claim was almost all worked out, Jackson's friend, partner and guide spotted another opportunity for the two of them:

"September 8, 1850: The gulch is getting narrow and there is a scant
fifty feet more before we reach the ditch. There is a flat of about a half
an acre where the gulch runs into the creek, and Anderson
says, the channel must run through it. If it does, we'll have at least
another month's work."

Anderson soon figured out a way to stake still a different kind of claim for the partnership:

"October 20, 1850: Anderson says it will be a good idea to extend our ditch and sell the water to miners who might want to use it. but i don't see what right we have got to it more than anybody else. Anyway, he has put a notice at the head of the ditch claiming all the water it will hold, and as there is no law in the case he says he will make a law out of precedent."

The claim that Jackson and Anderson staked on the flat turned out better than either of them had dreamed:

"March 23, 1851: It looks as if our flat is going to turn out to be a much bigger claim than we expected. The gravel, which is from two to four feet deep, pays pretty well and there are rich streaks on the bedrock that pan out big. If it holds out, we will have at least four months' more work."

In the end, this one claim yielded an astounding fortune for Jackson and his partner:

"June 1, 1851: "The claim pays regularly and it is almost certain that we will clean up ten or twelve thousand dollars apiece."

The gold miners weren't the only prospectors who staked claims. There were also the entrepreneurs who "mined the miners."

Throughout his diary, Jackson points out how various people found riches of another kind by serving the miners who searched for gold:

"May 19, 1850: All our letters come by mail to Sacramento and are then sent by express to Hamlet Davis, the storekeeper at Deer Creek, who acts as postmaster, although he has no legal appointment... Johnny Latham, the express rider, contracts to carry letters and papers for two bits each."

*"November 3, 1850: A minister preached in the United States Hotel
dining room and the place was filled...I was told he took
up a collection and raked in four hundred dollars. That is as
good as mining and not as hard work."*

In many respects, the people who served the miners did better
than the miners. The wealthiest man in California during
the early years of the Gold Rush was Samuel Brannan,
who was originally a shopkeeper and newspaper publisher.
As news of gold first broke, Brannan rushed to purchase all
the prospecting supplies – every pickaxe, shovel and pan –
available in San Francisco to later resell them to arriving
prospectors at a staggering profit. Brannan was the first one
to rush to cash in on the Gold Rush, only his version of gold
was the gear one needed to dig for gold.[9]

Other opportunists included the great barons who formed
the Central Pacific Railroad – Leland Stanford, Collis P.
Huntington, Mark Hopkins and Charles Crocker – all of
whom built their original wealth as Gold Rush merchants.
Stanford used part of his fortune to found California's most
prestigious university, eponymously named Stanford.[10]

Henry Wells and William Fargo opened Wells, Fargo & Co.
in 1852 in San Francisco. The services they offered included
buying and transporting gold and other valuables. Their
company is still alive and well today, and still headquartered
in San Francisco.[11] Their version of gold was the '49ers' need
to have gold converted into more portable currency, safely
stored and delivered to other places.

There are countless other names that we know today as
popular brand names, whose origins also trace to businesses
that profited from the Gold Rush. Consider Levi Strauss
(clothing), Armour (meats), Studebaker (wagons), Folgers
(coffee), Macy's (dry goods) and Ghirardelli (chocolate).[12] In

the opportunistic marketplace that was the Gold Rush, the path to success was the same regardless of where or what you were mining – you had to choose your spot, stake your claim, work your claim and defend your gains.

Like the Gold Rush, The Old Rush is going to create a whole new fast-moving and dynamic marketplace. Aging Baby Boomers will demand and pay a premium for as yet unimagined products and services, and movements in wealth will once again generate whole new ecosystems of opportunity.

To *participate* in this new landscape, you'll simply need to prioritize Boomers. (Congratulations, you've made it to San Francisco, but where exactly is the gold?) To *prosper*, you will need to get out there and prospect.

Prospecting is about exploring, discovering and making choices. Which Boomers should you reach? How should you reach them? What should you be to them? How do you make your space exclusive in a way that fences out competitors? This is all part of staking your claim and you'll want to do some groundwork to get a handle on these issues before you start the backbreaking work of digging.

Get to The Old Rush, find a promising place to dig, and start digging. That's the basic plan, and with a concentrated effort, success will eventually come. However, as with most things, once your experience grows, your technique improves. Success will come more easily and more substantially, and success will beget more success. In the next and final chapter of this section, we will focus on technique and the role that innovation played in accelerating gains in the Gold Rush. By definition, speed will continue to be the imperative for success in The Old Rush.

GOLD NUGGETS

FOLGERS COFFEE
– BROWN GOLD!

In my first job after college, I had the great
privilege of working at the **Cunningham & Walsh**
advertising agency on the **Folgers Coffee** account.
The brand was owned by **Procter & Gamble**
at that time. Folgers Coffee is another brand whose
origins trace back to the Gold Rush. The story starts
in Nantucket, which delights me, as this "faraway land"
has been a personal destination for much of my
adult life: a peaceful haven for inspiration,
relaxation and, of course, a little fishing.

In 1849, the Folger family sent three of its
sons west to California to seek their fortunes in gold.
The two older brothers went immediately into the
gold fields, but the youngest of the boys, James A.
Folger, didn't have enough money to travel any farther
than San Francisco. So it was there that he found a
job in order to get the travel funds he needed to get to
the gold. In 1850, James got a job with The Pioneer
Steam Coffee and Spice Mills. Pioneer would supply
miners with coffee already roasted, ground and
packed in tin containers.

By 1851, James had enough money to stake his claim,
and he set out for gold, also bringing along samples of

Pioneer's coffee and spices. He observed that the miners and prospectors were too busy to grind their coffee and, flush with new wealth, were willing to pay a bit more for coffee that was already roasted and ground. James suspended his dreams of riches from gold and took orders for Pioneer coffee instead. He made his way back to San Francisco and later became a full partner in the company. In 1872, he bought out the other partners and renamed it J.A. Folger & Company.[13]

CHAPTER
═══ TWELVE ═══

MINING FOR GOLD
Relying on natural tendencies.

**There are powerful demographic trends and
cultural forces that can be harnessed to help you
succeed in The Old Rush.**

I f a strong-willed '49er had thus far succeeded in getting
to California, gearing up and staking a claim, he was
no nearer to true success than when he first started if
he didn't have gold in hand. While he had positioned
himself to succeed, the most challenging task still lay ahead –
getting gold dust out of the ground.

In modern terms, the Gold Rush was an "emerging market,"
and as has been true of those marketplaces, success improves
only as one's learning curve improves.

If you look at the gear list of most of the early miners, it
included a pick, a shovel and a pan. Mining for gold was still
a new industry, and the early entrants had at best a very basic
understanding of technique and tools. As their experience
matured, their practices became a little more sophisticated
and yields improved over time.

When miners started out, they were panning. The pan
was essentially a heavy metal pie plate into which a miner
would add gravel and water, the latter being a catalyst for

separating the elements. The panner would then swirl the contents around, tilting the pan to let the water and the lighter materials drain out, leaving mainly gold and heavy black sand behind. A rocker was a step up from a pan. It was a simple but significant improvement in technology that simplified the process while also improving results.

A rocker, which resembled a baby's cradle, had a rounded perforated metal bottom that allowed water and dirt to pass through but stopped larger, worthless rocks. As the water and dirt washed through the rocker, heavier gold was trapped by a set of cleats.[14]

A rocker is yet another example of the ingenuity of the resourceful prospectors who showed up in California with exactly zero experience in mining gold. In the case of the rocker, they relied on something known to help them manage the unknowns of mining. A common baby's cradle was the inspiration for an extremely efficient and productive mining tool that was simple both to build and to use.

Another new innovation was known as the Long Tom. The Long Tom was structured along the lines of a large rocker, but was rocked by waterpower, not by hand. The river's own current provided the force and mechanical action needed to rock the Long Tom and to separate larger amounts of water, gravel and gold faster and more easily. The Long Tom represented the first mechanization in the gold fields, shifting mining from a hand activity to a mechanical one. The improvement in productivity for relatively simple miners like Jackson and Anderson was truly transformational.

After Jackson had built and installed a Long Tom, Anderson had yet another inspiration. He realized that in addition to washing gold out of gravel, a strong stream of water could also be used to directly wash the top layer of soil off the claim:

"August 18, 1850: We finished the ditch on Thursday and turned on the water....We pulled off our shoes, turned up our overalls, jumped into the trench and worked away like beavers, and the water did more work in one day than both of us could have stripped shoveling in a week."

Anderson's next big idea was to apply the same technique to the riverbed. In concept, this innovation would be more complicated and labor intensive, but it held enormous promise.

To pull this scheme off, Jackson and Anderson would need to get to work in late summer when the water level was at its lowest and work quickly before the fall rains arrived and worked against them:

"July 20, 1851: Pard is engineering the scheme and says that about the last of August it will be low water and then we will do some lively work wing damming the stream. He is sure that the bed of the river will pay big if we can get at it and stay in it long enough to clean up a good sized strip of it."

"October 19, 1851: We built a flume close up to the north side of the river and about three hundred feet from the head of our claims.... We put up a dam diagonally from the head of the claim to the head of the flume, turning all the water in the river through the flume. Then we built another dam at the foot of the flume to keep the backwater out, and that gave us a stretch of five hundred feet of riverbed fairly dry. We ran two Toms and three rockers steady."

The river project paid off almost as well as the flat on the creek:

"October 19, 1851: We worked both day and night, eight men in daylight, and six men at night. We will divide twenty-two thousand dollars, or about twenty-seven hundred and fifty dollars for each one of the company."

The innovation didn't stop, even after the highly lucrative river project. Jackson and Anderson even experimented with "drifting," which involved digging deep holes down through many layers of ground soil to find gold at the bedrock level. In the end, Jackson and Anderson were two ordinary men who experienced extraordinary success, mostly because they were relentlessly innovative.

One of the lessons learned from this aspect of the Gold Rush is that while innovation in any endeavor is both essential and perpetual, it need not be complex. Simple innovation just requires one to look differently at the assets already at hand, and to apply them to a new challenge in a new way.

The other lesson we've learned in this chapter is that gold, like people, has natural tendencies. Most of the mining innovation was built around the natural quality of gold – its density – and its natural tendency to separate from lighter materials.

The implication of both of these Gold Rush learnings is equally as simple: don't fight the natural tendency of things; use them to your advantage.

The next part of this book will offer insight and practical advice to help one succeed in that huge demographic, economic and social wave that we're calling The Old Rush. If you set your sights on success in The Old Rush, you will almost certainly meet resistance from the "natural tendency of things." As you strive to persevere, seek your inspiration from the '49ers. Every step of their journey to the gold presented a new challenge, but in the end, their success lay in their ability to use the inherent properties of existing things (gold and water) to their advantage.

Part Three will illuminate the natural tendencies of marketers and the Boomer consumer. For marketers, the bias toward the familiar, and for Boomers, the influential set of personal values instilled during their formative years.

Marketing for gold in the Age of Aging begins with getting at the fundamental human truths that shape relationships with brands. It is a journey to success that the dreamers won't begin and the ill-prepared won't finish. Instead, success will come to those who act first and who rely on their instincts to adapt along the way. The very best marketers in the business are instinctual because they respect their personal tendencies as well as those of the consumer. The Old Rush is about to begin – grab a pan and start making a plan.

(If you would like to read more of Jackson's diary, look up "diary of a forty-niner" on openlibrary.org.)

GOLD
NUGGETS

In **March 1848**, there were **fewer than 800 non-native Americans living in the California territory**. Twenty months later, following the initial Gold Rush migration, the **non-native population was more than 100,000**.[15]

More than 90,000 people went to California in the two years after the discovery of gold, and **more than 300,000** had arrived by **1854**. This was approximately **one** of every **90 people** then living in the United States.[16]

One out of every five miners who came to California in 1849 was **dead within six months**.[17]

PART

THREE

MARKETING FOR
GOLD IN THE
AGE OF AGING

CHAPTER
THIRTEEN

WHAT'S IN THE WAY
OF A NEW WAY?
Overcoming barriers to change.

Of the many recurring messages of this book, none is more relevant to marketing than the importance of acting quickly to achieve fast growth in emerging markets. U.S. Baby Boomers will "emerge" as a new post–eighteen to forty-nine cohort, having retained all of the potency and purchasing power that have made them Marketing's Most Valuable Generation™. The aging consumer is, and will continue to be, the most lucrative, nongeographic emerging market. The multinational marketers did not ignore the fast growth to be realized in the BRIC* markets, and they won't ignore the staggering upside in up-aging their marketing.

If you get this logic, you're probably starting to give some thought to a game plan for your brand or organization. As you mull your first move, you will want to start by identifying the things that might get in the way of the change that you will be advocating. Change is always hard, but there is nothing more exhilarating than change that leads to a real step-change in growth.

As you consider marketing to the aging consumer, the barriers that you will face will be personal, philosophical and

---

* Brazil, Russia, India, China

organizational. They are not unique to you or your market, but they will manifest themselves in different ways based on varying circumstances.

Let's start with you. It's important to ensure that you're ready enough to go the distance and to overcome the inevitable challenges along the way. Remember the miners – there was no expressway to the gold.

In founding BoomAgers, I faced a very similar first-mover opportunity, and challenge. I found inspiration in some wise words that are now engraved on an office plaque that I reinternalize every day: "What would you attempt if you knew you could not fail?" While enduring optimism had gotten me pretty far in advertising, I knew that I had to completely discard any notion of failure if I were to succeed in a new venture. Your challenge is the same. Believe in what you are advocating, and believe in yourself.

BoomAgers has been evangelizing the aging opportunity every hour of every day since the moment the company was started. We've seen and heard all of the commentary, and we've witnessed both action and inaction. Here's a firsthand summary of the philosophical and organizational challenges you can expect:

1. THE INERTIA OF THE STATUS QUO – We've all heard the anecdote about the boiled frog – despite the rising temperature of the water around him, the frog enjoys the comfort and warmth of his surroundings so much that he stays put and eventually meets a boiled fate. Change is always hard, but it's especially difficult when one's current situation is relatively comfortable.

From the day that the first Baby Boomer entered the eighteen to forty-nine marketing cohort, this target audience has become the coveted choice for most major advertisers. Marketing to this cohort typically met with great success. Beginning in 1964, nearly eighty million Boomers aged into the cohort. At the same time, all of Madison Avenue's philosophies, systems and processes were optimized around the eighteen to forty-nine target, making it easier and more predictable to validate advertising campaigns created for it. In short, eighteen to forty-nine became the comfortable choice for an entire generation of marketers who prospered from its size and love of brands.

To get your organization to set its sights on the aging, fifty-plus consumer, you will need to rethink the current choice of eighteen to forty-nine. In doing so, you will need to build a rational case, but you will also need to go up against the irrational power of inertia. Doing things the way they've always been done is comfortable, but it offers no guarantee of success.

2. BEST PRACTICES – Many marketing organizations pride themselves on their dedication to a set of best practices designed to be predictive of success. These best practices are typically created over time through the systematic searching and reapplying of earlier in-market successes. As new light is shed on an existing best practice, a new layer of understanding is applied, eventually creating a well-varnished approach to a given set of marketing circumstances.

Over time, best practices may deteriorate into intellectual inertia. Their essence is the belief that if it worked before, it will work again; the past is used as a predictor of the future. Best Practices are also seen as the ethos of a company's marketing culture – that is, "this is the way we do things here."

The weak link in the logic of best practices is change. If the future – by its very definition – brings change, then how can the past be used to effectively predict it? The future is here, and it has brought great change with it. Consider the effect of the following on best practice thinking:

Most of today's best practices are based on past experiences with an eighteen to forty-nine target audience that included eighty million Baby Boomers. In 2014, *all* of them will have aged out of this target. While it still *looks* like the eighteen to forty-nine audience, it's *acting* like a new audience.

If most all of today's marketing best practices were formed from an eighteen to forty-nine experience, then by default most of today's marketing organizations fundamentally lack best practices for a fifty-plus consumer. If their ethos is to use the past to predict the future, they do not yet have a past to apply.

The fifty-plus audience will probably act more like the original eighteen to forty-nine audience than the new eighteen to forty-nine one will. The key is to market to a consumer's set of values, which tend to endure irrespective of a person's age or stage in life.

Remember that every one of the '49ers lacked a best practice for participating in the Gold Rush. While the discovery of gold lacked a predictive precedent, it promised transformative wealth. That prospect stirred the resourceful spirit of the miners and encouraged them to substitute their lack of experience with ingenuity, creativity and perseverance.

3. FEAR OF THE UNKNOWN – Many marketing organizations also pride themselves on being "learning cultures." At the core of their culture is the relentless pursuit of new consumer and market knowledge. If knowledge is power, then these marketers make formidable competitors.

If for every action there's an opposite and equal reaction, then it's also true that these types of marketers abhor having gaps in their knowledge. When confronted with a knowledge outage, they have one of two choices: go out and learn about it or avoid it. A company's decision to avoid what it doesn't know usually reflects the following underlying logic: "If we're a true learning culture and we don't know this, then it must not be worth knowing." You would be amazed as to how many companies we have encountered whose management *assumes* that because their company doesn't know anything about the aging consumer, or isn't doing anything to learn more, those consumers must not be a valid business priority.

One of the biggest myths about older consumers is that they don't like technology. The truth is that many older consumers are technology enthusiasts. Preferences about technology are much more a function of personality than of age. Rather than make an assumption, ask your older customers how they would like to interact with your company. You might be surprised to discover how many Boomers like the convenience and privacy of being able to browse, select and order without having to deal with a salesperson.

4. OLD THINKING ABOUT "OLD" – Society and business alike are guilty of perpetuating unsubstantiated beliefs about "old" people. We live in a world where that which is new or young is preferred to that which is old. The subjective tendencies and biases of people are one thing, but smart businesses should really be seeking objective truths about the aging consumer.

The two erroneous beliefs that we hear most often are that a younger consumer is more valuable than an older consumer and that old people are set in their ways and won't switch brands.

According to U.S. census data, between now and 2030, the eighteen to forty-nine segment is expected to grow +12% whereas the fifty-plus segment will expand +34%. The same report indicates that by 2050, there will be 161 million fifty-plus consumers, +63% versus 2010.

Of these fifty-plus consumers, the Boomers own more than 70% of U.S. financial wealth, and their per capita income is 26% higher than the national average. They will account for over 50% of total retail spend by 2015, and they will continue to have robust purchasing power, as the majority (63%) of Boomer households still have at least one person in the household working full-time.[1]

As for allegedly being set in their ways, a 2012 BoomAgers study co-created with Nielsen analyzed twenty key product categories and found only minor variances in loyalty between age groups. Said another way, Boomers are no more or less brand loyal than their younger counterparts.[2]

Older consumers do not see themselves as "old" and neither should marketers. They see themselves as aging and changing, which is a natural life process and one that they believe actually brings improved quality of life. Boomers believe that they are actually getting better with age and that their best years of life are still ahead of them. Time has not passed them by, and neither should marketers.

Take a moment to think about all of the commercials you have seen on Viagra, Cialis and other medications that address erectile dysfunction. The couples in those commercials are always smiling, vital and ready to enjoy themselves. They aren't surrendering to age; they're ready to take a pill and keep going. That's a typical Boomer attitude.

5. PAINTING BY NUMBER – In 1950, when the first of the Boomers were still young children, Max S. Klein brought to market painting by number kits to help introduce them to art.[3] For years since, those in the advertising creative profession have used "painting by number" as a sobriquet to describe overly prescriptive client feedback to their "works of art."

This aside, marketing has in fact become more methodical over the years, just as business itself has. The best practices we spoke of earlier don't live in the absolute – they live in the context of a methodical marketing process built to deliver efficient consistency of result. The best process strives to make decision making as objectively black and white as possible, shunning gray areas, and certainly colorful judgment; instinct has been expunged in favor of "informed" decision making.

Our successful '49ers persevered despite contending with the reverse of this paradigm – a lot of instinct substituting for little or no information. The same will be true in The Old Rush – instinct is going to need to be crucial to process because the process for marketing to the aging consumer is still a blank canvas.

6. RISK AND REWARD – The original Gold Rush was an example of a risk/reward trade-off. If you were willing to put it all on the line, you stood a very good chance of being handsomely rewarded. Risk was seen as a good thing, as it was a means to a very positive end.

Today, Wall Street's demand for consistent and predictable results has made risk a bad thing. Risk is anathema to big, publicly financed companies. Risk, they rationalize, is the purview of start-ups and entrepreneurs who have fewer assets to risk. True, but how often have you heard a struggling, established firm challenge its people to be "more entrepreneurial"? These are the same companies that popularized the operating strategy known as "risk management."

In theory, managing risk means striking an acceptable balance between risk and reward so as to enable success. In practice, it has become more about minimizing risk so as to prevent failure. In companies in which this is happening, it's usually because the employees do not feel any direct relationship between their personal risk and their personal reward. If taking on additional risk leads only to the same reward, then it's not a risk worth taking. Survival trumps paramount to success.

The Old Rush is all about success, and those companies that are focused on it have shifted to a model of reward management in lieu of risk management. They are eliminating the risk of a status quo approach in favor of the reward associated with new choices.

All of these Old Rush challenges have one thing in common, which they also share with the Gold Rush. Each represents *the familiar*. Every '49er who moved west had to leave something behind, referred to earlier as their metaphorical East. While each of them left many different things behind, they were all *familiar* things that were exchanged for the unfamiliar requirements of prospecting for gold. The miners were willing to step outside of the comfort zone of the familiar because the potential for reward far outweighed the risk. If you want your company to be a first mover in The Old Rush, you will need to overcome the inertia of the familiar. The only way to accomplish this is to define risk and reward differently, and to strike a new balance between them. In The Old Rush, risk is the missed opportunity of doing nothing combined with the threat of competition doing it first. Reward is the fast growth associated with being first in an emerging market and the ability to own a preemptive position in perpetuity. As marketing becomes more and more complex, there will be fewer opportunities as straightforward as The Old Rush. It's time to spread the word.

GOLD
NUGGETS

A MODEL BOOMER

"I've loved my generation," says Cindy Joseph,
"I'm a classic Boomer. Born in '51. Grew up in
middle-class America in a suburban home." She continues
to love her generation and her age so much so that
she recently created "Boom! By Cindy Joseph," a line
of Pro-Age Natural Cosmetics.

Cindy spent much of her working life in the background,
doing the makeup for top models and actors being shot
by the very best photographers. She knew every trick and
technique for making people look younger than they were,
because that's what her clients wanted.

When she was forty-nine, she decided to stop
coloring her own hair, which is now a radiant silver.
On the day that she cut off the last of the dyed hair
so she could be completely natural, she was approached on
a New York City sidewalk by a scout who asked if
she would consider being a model in a campaign for a
fashion designer. Cindy thought it was a prank. She was
sure she wasn't young enough or tall enough to be a
model. The scout had to repeat the question several times
before Cindy finally took her seriously.

That first assignment led to years of modeling as a
prestigious Ford model. Cindy has a distinctive attitude

about it all. She tells everyone who wants to hire her that she is available only if they're ready to take her as she is: no dying her hair and making her look younger. This natural commitment to her natural looks seemed to make even more people want to hire her.

"When I thought about how reluctant I was to believe that anyone wanted to use me as a model," she says, "I realized that I had a huge prejudice, because I grew up in the business. I knew what a model was supposed to be and it was not a forty-nine-year-old, silver-haired woman." She countered her prejudice by becoming deliberately optimistic about aging. This is reflected in her state of mind: "I'm happier than I've ever been in my life, healthier than I've ever been in my life, smarter, more educated, more skilled, wiser. You can only get better."

When she heard that women had started asking questions online about what kind of makeup she wore, she recognized a business opportunity and a way to share her sense of the beauty of aging. Boom! Cosmetics don't cover or conceal; they nourish and enhance. For many Boomer women, this is a welcome new wrinkle.

CHAPTER
═══ FOURTEEN ═══

GENERATIONAL MARKETING
*A "new age" approach
to marketing to age.*

I t's one thing to recognize that aging Boomers represent a great business opportunity, but it's another thing altogether to figure out *how* to take advantage of that with marketing. One thing is for sure, though – you won't be able to succeed by simply doing what you've always done. Just as Maslow's Law of the Hammer posits that it's narrow-minded to use one tool for many purposes, don't expect that the tools and processes used for younger consumers will be productive with aging consumers. You'll need new tools and know-how to market to age in the new age of marketing.

Nothing dominates today's new-age marketing conversation more than modern connection tactics. In a business that has always coveted that which is new and different, we now find ourselves infatuated with all of the cutting-edge communications tools spawned by digital technology and the proliferation of screens. Clickstreams, cache bursting, interstitials? Each comes complete with its own new language, adding still more complexity as if only to shift the power of knowledge to the technologically fluent.

At a recent advertising industry convention, the chief marketing officer of the world's largest advertiser delivered a call to action to the agency community, imploring them to forget the clever technology and to fall back in love with big ideas. His message resonates. Although the names have changed, the fundamental tenets of marketing remain unchanged – marketing is still about executing timeless themes in timely ways. It's still about big ideas, and the core communication imperative continues to be one of connecting with your target consumer when and where he/she will be most receptive to your message.

Therefore, when we speak to the need for new tools and new know-how for communicating with aging consumers, we're proposing new and timely ways of executing timeless themes.

For starters, this means getting a timely understanding of what makes Boomers receptive to your brand's core value proposition. Simply put, getting them to respond to *your* value proposition requires that you understand *their* values.

A person's values are his or her set of personal beliefs accumulated through a lifetime of experiences. These values guide one's behavior and form the basis for personal integrity and ethics. Said another way, values are the foundation of one's being and, as such, they tend to endure for a lifetime.

While values seem like a very relevant tool, most marketing is dedicated to demographics. A target audience is defined, targeted and measured numerically, beginning with age.

Other approaches look for relevance in a consumer's lifestage. This approach is based on the premise that consumers develop new and unique lifestyle needs as they enter into new life phases (e.g., a young mother's first baby).

Both of these models – age and stage – dominates today's marketing, but they have inherent limitations when applied to the aging consumer.

Age is a very tempting way to target aging consumers. However, the logic of this rationale typically breaks down in practice in one of two ways. First, targeting a group of consumers by using a common metric like age makes the assumption that the age-based cohort is monolithic – that all of the consumers are the same and will act the same. This approach flies in the face of what we fundamentally know about Boomers – they are a collection of individuals who celebrate their differences and defy mass definition.

Second, being age-specific is tempting because it's usually a neat and tidy solution for organizing a brand's offerings. This approach may work in some categories – especially those where product and packaging nomenclature is complex – but more often than not it has a stigmatizing effect. Aging consumers know they're aging but they don't want to be explicitly identified by a chronological age.

The logic of stage-based targeting is equally compelling. While understanding the new needs that emerge at new stages of one's life is absolutely essential, *how* that understanding is leveraged in marketing is critical. In speaking to a consumer's new stage, one must be very careful not to overtly signal that the consumer has an *age*-based need. Stage-based promises are okay as long as the stage does not imply age.

Given that the traditional age- and stage-based targeting models pose issues for targeting aging consumers, there's need for a new model: Generational Marketing. In this model, one markets to a consumer's generational values – personal beliefs that endure irrespective of his or her age or stage. Generational values guide behavior and brand choices, and when you truly understand them and can tap into them, you can make authentic connections that help your brand to genuinely improve the consumer's life.

People who have shown a lifelong interest in learning by taking courses, going on educational cruises, attending lectures and reading new books don't suddenly lose their urge to learn when they turn fifty. They can be interested in buying everything from museum memberships to online courses. And one of the best ways to bring a product to their attention is in the context of an educational experience..

When we founded BoomAgers, we made generational marketing core to our capabilities, as it is a new and necessary tool for marketing in the new age of marketing. This approach also helped us to address two other challenges that marketers face when targeting a massive and misunderstood cohort like the Boomers. First, it put the need for consumer understanding (e.g., values) at the core of our creative process, and second, it provided the foundation for a segmentation model that helps us to identify specific groups of Boomers that have differing potential based on their differing values.

Our inspiration for this model comes from a sociological approach called "generational cohort theory" that maintains that events, social change and pop culture affect the values, beliefs, attitudes and ultimately the behavior of individuals. In this framework, a generation is less about the age of the group and more about its members' shared experiences, especially those from their youth. Recall our specific look at this in Part One, in which we learned about the influential post-war cultural context in which today's aging consumers came of age.

From there, we partnered with a leading consumer intelligence company to scientifically segment Boomers by their unique value-driven mind-sets. This led to some fascinating differentiating descriptions of this massive cohort, summarized in the chart given later in this chapter. To illuminate how this model comes to life, let's take a look at a couple of segments, beginning with Medonism.

This segment represents 14% of Boomers and has an egocentric, hedonistic approach to life. Their prevailing belief is that life is for living and their values are oriented to pleasure, entitlement, freedom, happiness and joy. Remember the hedonistic flame that burned so brightly in the 1960s and 1970s? It's still burning in these aging Boomers, who still believe that "if it feels good, do it."

By contrast, the Higher Consciousness segment represents 18% of Boomers and has a spiritually driven approach to life. Their dominant belief is that balance is the key to a harmonious existence, and their values are all about religion, order, stability, affiliation and relationships. These are the Boomers who found a deeper meaning of life and have a more balanced and grounded approach to their choices.

Now imagine that you are a financial services provider looking to sell retirement savings products to Boomers. This would be a smart target choice, as most Boomers are still actively generating income while also realizing that their current savings may be insufficient for an extended life. If you took an age-based approach to target them, you would be pursuing a mass-audience play that assumes that because they are all of the same age, they all have the same attitudes about saving money and planning for the future and will therefore have similar propensities for choosing your retirement product.

If you instead looked at this through a generational, values-based lens, a different picture would emerge. Using only the two segments that we have illuminated – Medonism and Higher Consciousness – it becomes immediately clear that one target is a much better choice than the other. A Medonist lives in the moment and believes that hard-earned money is a reward that should be spent on pleasure. Immediate gratification is his/her financial strategy because,

BoomAgers	% of Boomers	Focus	Belief	Values
MEDONISM	14%	Personal	My life is for living	Pleasure Entitlement Freedom Happiness Joy
FOREVER YOUNG	22%	Emotional	Age is not a number, it is a long life without limitations	Optimism Prosperity Competence Security Peace of Mind
ME MY BODY	12%	Physical	A healthy body is the key to a productive life	Health Development Physicality Accomplishment
HIGHER CONSCIOUSNESS	18%	Spiritual	Balance is the key to a harmonious existence	Religion Order Stability Affiliation Relationships
MIND EXPANSION	19%	Intellectual	Life is a continuous learning experience	Change Improvement Wisdom Knowledge Responsibility
RAGS TO RICHES	15%	Material	Accomplishment is the measure of one's success	Hard Work Competition Wealth Recognition Achievement

Source: BoomAgers in partnership with
The Natural Marketing Institute

hey, you can't take it with you, right? There's more than a good chance that they aren't all that interested in a sales pitch to set aside money for later when it can be so well spent now.

On the other hand, Higher Consciousness consumers tend to lead a more balanced, structured life. They have a plan, and because they embrace order and stability, they have the discipline that it takes to make sacrifices in the short term to ensure a sustainable quality of life. If you're selling retirement savings products, the Higher Consciousness consumer is going to be much more interested in what you're selling.

Continuing with our simple two-segment evaluation, let's assume that our financial services provider decides to target the Higher Consciousness consumer. A brand manager with a mass-marketing orientation might dismiss this choice, as it only has our financial company targeting 18% of the audience. True, but it's important to remember that this would be 18% of eighty million, a massive number in and of itself. Further, as we have learned by taking a deep look at their values, it is an audience with much higher savings potential. Given that we live in the new age of marketing, we now have the advantage of marketing tools that are much more precise. Our fictitious financial company can now create a highly customized message – written specifically to the values of the Higher Consciousness target – that can be digitally addressed to them when and where they are most apt to be receptive. The campaign would probably position the retirement savings product as a way to achieve a financial balance that would underpin security.

Once that company had thoroughly penetrated and developed the Higher Consciousness Boomers, they might again look at the segments to see where additional opportunity might be. If they decided to approach the Rags to Riches Boomers, they would be wise to create a totally different campaign that positioned investing in the retirement savings product as an achievement.

As you can see, the generational targeting model led to not only a more precise understanding of the target consumer but also the opportunity to create and deliver a hypertargeted and, therefore, hypereffective message. While this type of model can be applied to any of the other adult generations, it is particularly compelling when used for Boomers, given that the large overall size of the cohort results in segments sizable enough to deliver a meaningful business result.

While using this model to its fullest can be a fairly complex, sophisticated process, you can probably see how it could help inform marketing decisions in almost any category. The Me My Body segment, for example, would be a good target for a fitness club that wanted active members. If the club wanted people who would buy a membership and not use the club too often, they could market to Medonists. If you were marketing frozen meals, you might decide to tell Me My Body Boomers about healthy ingredients. On the other hand, you could tell Medonists how convenient frozen meals are.

When executed well, a message inspired by an understanding of the target consumer's values is almost always going to result in more authentic, effective communications. Authenticity is critical, given that Boomers are not only the most valuable generation in marketing but also the savviest and most experienced consumers. This is true by virtue of the fact that they have been on the receiving end of more media and more messaging for longer than any other target. They are going to hold your brand to a higher standard, not because they are cynical but because they demand more from the brands they have loved for so long.

In summary, if personal values are core to one's being, then they need to be core to your efforts to influence choice and improve people's lives with your products and services. This is especially true, if not essential, with an aging consumer whose values have been well defined over time.

As essential as this approach is, it is not an end unto itself – it is simply a means of getting at a deeper, initial consumer understanding.

In subsequent chapters, we will share further insight into the complexities of aging that will highlight the need for still deeper understanding of this unique consumer. Much of the established theory and process around marketing is rational, but the human response to aging is irrational. If one attempts to apply typical, rational approaches to a market dynamic that is fundamentally irrational, the opportunity for a disconnect is almost certain. Just as you will need to balance the rational with the irrational, you will also need to find harmony between the disciplines of art and science that are at the heart of creative marketing. Success will lie in your ability to bring art to the interpretation of science, and science to the art of creating ideas.

GOLD
NUGGETS

APPEALING,
AGE-FRIENDLY DESIGN

Tucker Viemeister, a Boomer, is one of the gurus of industrial, product and experiential design. He speaks humbly and plainly about what he does and tends to share credit for his accomplishments with his team members and clients. It seems almost as if he doesn't realize how remarkable his work is because it is the result of his thinking the way he naturally thinks.

Over years of working on everything from kitchen gadgets to computer interfaces, he has evolved his own ideas about designing for aging people. His ideas, stated from a design perspective, are akin to BoomAgers' ideas from a marketing perspective. Tucker sees aging populations as more diverse than younger ones. "Aging isn't really chronological," he says. "It's how you get more and more specific. Kids are all talking about the same thing: sex or whatever. Older people have different physical issues going on."

Tucker also intuitively understands that it just makes good sense to provide aging people with first-rate products. Early in his career he met someone who had studied gerontology and who was designing products for older populations. He asked, "Why are you making stuff for old people that looks stupid and frumpy?

Why not make good-looking stuff for old people?"
Tucker got a chance to put this thinking into action
when he was part of the team at the New York industrial
design group Smart Design that responded to Sam
Farber's request that they design a potato peeler that
would be easier for his wife Betsy, who had mildly
arthritic hands, to use. Here's how he tells that story:

"One of the team members, an ergonomics
specialist, pointed out that a bigger handle would
be easier to hold and provide more leverage. I had
gone to a focus group on a new plastic, Santoprene,
that could be formulated to allow you to adjust how
rubbery it was. The team thought this would help
create a better handle."

"The plastic not only made the handle softer,
but it also provided friction so it was easier
to hold on to it. You held on to the handle
better with much less force. Then we put little fins
on it to make it even more mushy where your
thumb went. Those fins signaled to people that this
was going to be comfortable and ergonomic and
this was going to be easier to hold. It turned out that the
fins were more of a symbol than functional. But they
helped give the peeler a distinctive look."

"We designed the handle, and then we realized
that we couldn't sell it as a potato peeler for
handicapped people. No handicapped person would
want to buy one. They don't want to be told they
need a handicapped peeler."

"The idea of designing cool stuff for old people plus
the realization that you couldn't sell enough of a product
that was specifically for handicapped people made us
realize that there was this idea of Universal Design.

If you designed stuff for old people and made it cool enough, everybody would like it."

The potato peeler was the start of Oxo's Good Grips line of kitchen tools. The line made its debut at the Gourmet Products Show in San Francisco in 1990 and soon proved that consumers were ready to pay a significant premium for its age-friendly, superior, ergonomic design.

Tucker is eager to focus his ever-active mind on designing homes and facilities that are beautiful and age-friendly. "If you think ahead," he says, "you can design stuff that will be more accessible for everybody. For example, if you make a building closer to the ground, you won't need steps or ramps."

CHAPTER
═══ FIFTEEN ═══

GETTING BETTER WITH AGE
Navigating the psychological complexities of aging.

If you're a wine collector, you probably know that 1959 was and remains one of the finest vintages ever produced in the Bordeaux region of France, home to some of the most sought-after wines in the world. Like these wines, I too was "born" in 1959, and as a Boomer, I too believe that I am aging like a fine wine, getting better by the year. Herein lies one of the greatest paradoxes of marketing to the aging consumer.

In an earlier chapter, we cautioned about the risk in perpetuating "old thinking about old." One of the most frequent manifestations of this way of thinking is to regard aging as a biological process that is measured chronologically. It's okay for gerontologists to think this way, but it's pure peril for a marketer.

As a marketer, you need to set aside the biology of aging and embrace the psychology of aging, which is fundamentally irrational. It's not enough to understand how they are changing physically, as you will also need to understand how they are reacting to the process of aging. It is this reaction – mostly psychological – that leads to a new set of attitudes and behavior.

So why is something that is scientific so irrational? Simple. The scientific part of aging is scary – impending death is not a pleasant thought. Human nature compensates by rationalizing aging in irrational ways that are more pleasing. This is what we mean by the psychology of aging.

The psychology of aging manifests itself in some unique philosophies on aging. Here's a quick description of Boomers' attitudes toward aging:

"How could I be getting older if I feel so young?"

Every Boomer feels younger than his/her biological age, and the older Boomers get, the younger they feel.

Most Boomers believe that "old age" starts at seventy-two, and 50% say they feel ten years younger than their age. [4] 33% of those who are sixty-five to seventy-four say they feel ten to nineteen years younger than their age. [5]

At our agency, we have a rule of thumb to refer to the psychological postponement of aging – we call it the "the +20 paradigm of aging." It goes as follows: ask a thirty-year-old what "old" is and he will answer "fifty." Ask a fifty-year-old and he will respond with "seventy." Said another way, a fifty-year-old believes he is young, and if you're smart, you'll market to the age that consumers *believe* that they are. This propensity to constantly redefine old age as one approaches old age recently led the cartoonist Garry Trudeau to quip that "dead is the new old."

"I'm not aging, I'm just changing."

Most of today's consumer packaged goods (CPG) marketers are in the business of creating superior-performing products that meet unmet consumer needs. Their orientation is need-centric, and their consumer learning process is built to seek out problems or issues that current products don't address. They seek out problems so as to design solutions, which has led to a popular format of advertising used for decades: problem/ solution.

The Boomers grew up with these kinds of ads. Who could forget classics like "Hate that gray?/Wash it away with Clairol," or "Those dirty rings around the collar/Wisk around the collar beats ring around the collar," or "Dishpan hands/ Use Palmolive?"

In marketing to the aging consumer, the problem with the problem/solution approach is the problem itself. Aging Boomers don't see themselves as having problems. Yes, unexpected things do happen as part of aging, but it's much more pleasant to rationalize them as changes, i.e., normal things that happen as one's body changes. As a generation that was born during a time of unprecedented optimism, it's only natural for them to avoid the negativity of problems in preference for a positive outlook on age-related developments.

"I'm happier than I've ever been."

There is scientific evidence that people get happier as they get older. While there are differing theories as to why this is, most agree that later-life contentedness is the combined result of accumulated wisdom and confidence as well as a general acceptance of aging. Older people are at a stage in life where they can reflect on their positive life experiences and savor their accomplishments. The anxiety associated with striving is replaced by the satisfaction of a life well lived.

Further, we've also learned that as quantity of life decreases, emphasis on quality of life increases. Each and every day matters, and with increased discretionary time, Boomers are intent on experiencing all of the enjoyable things that a busy lifestyle had postponed. They have the means to afford quality products and services and they relish discovering the new experiences that they offer.

Yes, there is joy in aging. While this is incomprehensible to younger marketers, it's greeted with knowing nods by aging people. Aging is change, and if you're an optimist, change brings opportunity.

In addition to these attitudes toward aging, there are lifestyle dynamics that are influencing how Boomers make brand choices in the "Age of Aging." Here are four of the themes that will have the most significant influence:

1. WELL-BEING – Physical, emotional and spiritual well-being will be central to happiness and productivity in the Age of Aging. The Boomers are taking better care of themselves, living longer and staying more active than any generation in history. They are extending their lives and enhancing their lifestyles. Their goal is to age while enjoying a life without compromise.

Despite the expectation of uncompromised living, millions of Boomers will need to confront the physical consequences of aging. Marketers are preparing with a dizzying array of "anti-aging" products. But the key to their success is not the product alone – they will also need to understand the psychology of aging.

Although Boomers know they're getting old, they don't want to be told that they're old. They're seeking empathy, understanding and a decidedly positive portrayal of their life. Brands need to understand them and demonstrate this with real, authentic communication.

2. SIMPLICITY AND STREAMLINING – The complexity of life has increased exponentially. Paradoxically, as we enter the

Age of Aging, the reverse is likely to be true.

Two dynamics are converging to create this effect – technology is simplifying our lives at the same time that eighty million Boomers are aging and seeking streamlined lifestyles – simplifying their lives because they want to and they can afford to.

As Boomers are confronted with imposing "modern realities," they will compensate by choosing to experience them on their own terms. Whether it's the latest smart phone, operating system, photo-sharing service, blog, social platform, e-book or cloud-based whatever, Boomers will choose to use what accommodates and respects their need for plug-and-play simplicity. In pursuit of a simpler life, Boomers will eschew Millennial multitasking. More than half of all Boomers are now on Facebook, but their usage is "by appointment," not "always on." For Boomers, simplicity equates to quality of life.

3. GROWTH – The Boomers are not getting older – they're *growing* older. They are defying the unrelenting progress of aging with a determination to continue to learn and grow. It is only the "afternoon" of their lives and there's still much to be accomplished. Boomers are continuing, not stopping, and the virtues of lifelong growth have reemerged.

For brands and marketers, "growth" is a growth business. Boomers love to discover, and they will pay a premium for products and services that can help sustain their physical, intellectual, emotional and spiritual growth.

4. HOME-CENTRICITY – The Baby Boom generation is retiring at a rate of 10,000 per day, a trend that will continue unabated for the next seventeen years. The "me-centric" generation is about to become the "home-centric" generation. The time and resources that once were spent commuting and at work are being reallocated to a home-based daily lifestyle. New, home-centric patterns of living will have a huge impact on the consideration and usage of an endless array of products and services.

Let's take a look at how these themes might affect product usage patterns and brand choice, focusing on home-centricity. Let's think about coffee. Coffee consumption patterns are going to change radically as Boomers retire from the workplace and spend more time at the homeplace.

For all of the years that an average Boomer was commuting to a job, the first cup of coffee in the morning was likely to be a hurried one, perhaps grabbed on the go and finished in the car. If a second or third cup was part of their daily habit, they were most likely purchased and consumed at the workplace.

Now, if we assume that a commute to an off-site workplace is no longer part of the daily routine and that our Boomer will still have two or three cups of coffee each morning, we can suppose that some, if not all, of that coffee will be made and consumed at home. Think of the implications for producers of coffee and coffee-making products.

For most people, coffee is more than just a beverage. It is the center of a variety of personal and interpersonal rituals and is deeply experiential. As Boomers restart with a new home-centric lifestyle, they will develop new and different coffee rituals. This is a classic stage-based opportunity. If you're a marketer of home-centric coffee products, how might you generate trial and loyalty as part of these new consumer rituals? For the answer, let's revisit the segmentation model that we shared earlier.

For this exercise, we've arrayed the five highest-potential

Boomer segments in relation to the top coffee category benefits: taste and aroma, wakes me up, helps me focus, day brightening, and warmth and intimacy. This creates a portfolio of opportunity that helps us to identify the best target segment vis-à-vis the category benefit that's most relevant for it.

For the Boomers in the Medonism segment, coffee is seen as a source of personal pleasure, and that pleasure is viscerally derived from taste and aroma. For them, coffee is a simple pleasure to start *their* day.

Those in the Forever Young category respond to emotional triggers with an optimistic outlook. Their morning cup of coffee is an opportunity to ponder the day with a confident outlook. Coffee is a source of optimism and their attitude is *carpe diem!*

For the Me My Body Boomers, coffee is all about its physical effects. They use coffee as a tool to wake themselves up and to jump-start their engines. You'll want to think of coffee as fuel for their high-performance "engines."

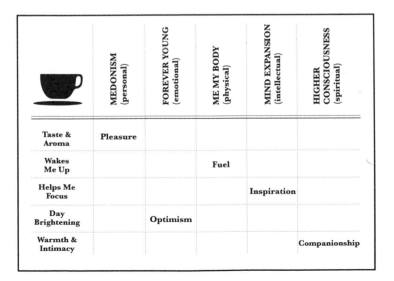

	MEDONISM (personal)	FOREVER YOUNG (emotional)	ME MY BODY (physical)	MIND EXPANSION (intellectual)	HIGHER CONSCIOUSNESS (spiritual)
Taste & Aroma	Pleasure				
Wakes Me Up			Fuel		
Helps Me Focus				Inspiration	
Day Brightening		Optimism			
Warmth & Intimacy					Companionship

The Mind Expansion Boomers think of coffee in a more intellectual way. They want their cup of coffee to sharpen their senses and make them more present and aware. Coffee is a source of inspiration that helps them to be at their best all day long.

Higher Consciousness Boomers look at coffee, and indeed, everything they consume, as part of their spiritual experience and journey. Their focus is on the warmth and intimacy that they experience while drinking coffee. For them, coffee stirs their soul.

What's fascinating about this approach is the fact that the same cup of coffee can be many different things to different people. Most all of mass marketing theory and practice is about the search for *universal* truths. One target audience, one insight, one strategy. It is all about common denominators.

By contrast, when you apply segmentation to a marketing opportunity, you are fundamentally looking for *variability*. How do these different people differ and how does one need to position their product differently to appeal to them? As mentioned earlier, this can lead to a Boomer-targeting strategy that prioritizes only the highest-potential segments, understood via hypersensitive insights and reached with hypereffective messaging.

In Part Two, we spoke of the natural tendencies of gold, and the ways in which prospectors used them to their advantage. The message of this chapter is very similar, in that the tendency of aging people is to resist the negativity of aging by rationalizing it as something positive. This type of rationalization is fundamentally irrational, but it is nonetheless the "natural" way that Boomers deal with aging. In the same way that they have redefined aging as a psychological coping strategy, you will need to redefine aging and reframe the benefits of your products and services accordingly. You will need to do some of your own rationalizing, by rethinking that which you manufacture versus that which you're selling.

GOLD
NUGGETS

THE BOOMER MUSIC MAN

Bob Farnsworth, a Boomer, believes that the majority of today's commercials are off-key and off-pitch for Boomer consumers. You probably haven't heard of Bob, but you've heard his work. He's President/Composer at Hummingbird Productions in Nashville, Tennessee, the music house that created the sound of the famous Budweiser frogs. Bob passionately believes that most advertising agencies today place too much emphasis on "cool" sounds and ideas that they think will impress young consumers at the expense of the humor, melody, simplicity, story, branding and hummability that Boomers grew up with and love.

Bob illustrates his point by singing a few jingles from his childhood: "Oh I wish I was an Oscar Mayer weiner"; "Like a good neighbor, State Farm is there" (written by Barry Manilow); "Nationwide is on your side" (written by the legendary jingle king Steve Karmen). Each song is firmly attached to a brand. When he sings, "I'd like to teach the world to sing," every Boomer within earshot thinks "Coke," even though Bob has not yet sung the brand name. Each of the jingles brings a smile to the face of listening Boomers. These sound signatures continue to deliver massive returns on investments made long ago. Bob finds it difficult to believe that so few marketers continue to leverage this ever-fresh approach.

"I'm so on the same page with BoomAgers," Bob says, "on this whole thing. If you get to the end of a commercial and the viewer can't remember who it was for, you have failed. Common sense. It's as if some of the younger marketers are deliberately trying to lose their Baby Boomer consumers."

As a professional running a business, Bob follows his clients' directions and helps them realize their creative visions, whether or not they sound like what Bob would have done. Even then, he is often able to use his expertise to make a commercial better for Boomers. He can recommend changes so that the sound track will be more comprehensible and less irritating for Boomers who, as a natural part of aging, lose the ability to hear the higher ranges.

His advice is relatively simple. Don't have a track that is competing too strongly with the lyrics. Don't make the accompaniment too confusing. Don't have the lyrics move too quickly. His last bit of advice in this area can be a revelation because it seems counterintuitive. "Don't make it too loud, he says. "That diminishes overall ability to hear."

While Bob can help make the sound of almost any commercial better, in his heart of hearts, he wishes that more markets would think about the effect of the joy and pleasure that music triggers deep in listeners' minds and how to leverage that effect. "In order to brand," he notes, "you need to jog people's memories...which means using melody."

"We have a culture of advertising people," he says, "who are advertising to the public as if the only people who matter are thirty-five and younger." He believes this is totally unnecessary, because it is possible to create music that everybody can relate to. To underscore his point, he sings the tune of "Sweet Georgia Brown" and then asks, "Now who doesn't like that?"

CHAPTER
SIXTEEN

PERFUME OR HOPE?
Know what you're really selling.

In a classic moment of revelation, Charles Revson, the founder of Revlon, once said, "In the factory I bottle perfume and in the department store I sell hope." His understanding of the purest essence of perfume launched a global cosmetic empire that thrives to this day. Grand, but simple at the same time. All of us in marketing need to have a pithy understanding of the true essence of what we are *really* selling, but especially if you're selling to the aging consumer. If they're changing the way they think about themselves, then you will need to change the way you think about your brand.

One of the ways to position a product to a target of Boomers is to present it in a new context. In marketing, we refer to this process as "reframing." To follow the analogy, an existing piece of art is presented with a new frame on it, creating the impression that the art itself has also changed. Reframing gives the consumer a new, or refreshed, way of looking at an existing product or service.

Done the right way, reframing can be truly transformative. Some of the greatest business innovators in recent years have been brilliant reframers who developed new ways for thinking differently about their businesses.

Let's continue with coffee. Howard Schultz is the innovator behind the phenomenal success of Starbucks. His reframe was to think about the coffee shop not as a store that sells coffee but as a new place in people's lives. He called it the "third place," a new place equal in importance to people's first and second places (i.e., home and work). Starbucks stores were designed to encourage people to linger, not to maximize throughput. And, knowing that coffee was so often the center of rituals, Schultz made sure that Starbucks baristas had a distinct vocabulary for their products. The myriad of options possible when ordering a coffee made sure that consumers had personal involvement in the making of their Starbucks coffee.

Richard Branson, the maverick adventurer behind Virgin Airlines, used his creativity to reframe air travel. Previously, airlines had branded themselves by attempting to differentiate their in-flight experience. This was natural. The flight was their product, but the ability to meaningfully differentiate in this space was limited. To break out of this trap, Branson decided to identify and address the primary "irritant" in the category, the aspect of the flying experience that was bothering his customers the most. The chief consumer irritant was not something in the plane; it was the hassles of getting to and from the plane.

Branson responded by thinking of Virgin Air's product in a broader frame. He decided that the Virgin product was not just the gate-to-gate flight experience, but also the customer's door-to-door travel experience. He made door-to-door car service part of the New York to London Virgin air experience.

Over the course of my career in advertising, I have had my own share of success with reframing, notably on the Progresso soup brand, then owned by Pillsbury. Progresso made a great soup, but it had the formidable challenge of going up against the quintessential and well-entrenched Campbell's brand; Progresso was a mere David about to clash with a Goliath.

At the heart of our reframe was the philosophy of "repositioning the competition." In this approach, it's not enough to merely position one's brand; it must be positioned in a way that also repositions the competition. At the heart of the Campbell's position was its historic equity of childhood. There is not a consumer out there who doesn't associate Campbell's with the warmth their mother provided after a cold day outdoors during their childhood. You remember the ads – the building of a snowman followed by mom's greeting at the door and a bowl of steaming Campbell's soup.

To reposition Campbell's from this position of strength, we came up with an advertising campaign that converted childhood to childish. The campaign asked Campbell's users why they were still eating the soup they ate as a kid if they were now grown-ups and had a better choice. The ads positioned Progresso as the Adult Soup and generated leadership results in the ready-to-eat soup category for years to come.

More recently, we started a meeting at P&G by saying, "There are two things we never do at BoomAgers. We don't use numbers and we don't use colors." We were about to have a conversation about aging, and we wanted to make it clear that marketers need a new way to frame their existing image of aging, which is typically defined by chronology or color. This cleared the way for a reframe and a new set of language and terminology that led to new methodologies.

To use a hypothetical example relevant to aging, imagine that you are a marketer of toothpaste. Your consumer learning has probably revealed that aging consumers are experiencing new dental issues as their mouths age. Gums recede, saliva production decreases and bacteria levels increase. The temptation might be to position a variant of your toothpaste as a fifty-plus version, borrowing a page from the vitamin category. However, if you were to consider a reframe, you might instead introduce new products that offered the benefit of "Oral Revitalization." You will know that they are optimized to address the new things happening in an aging consumer's mouth, but to the aging consumer, the products will be openly received as smart products that will help their mouths stay great. There's that old saying that goes, "If you always do what you've always done, you'll always get what you've always got." At BoomAgers, we paraphrase this with our dedication to "working differently to get different work," and the same mantra should be true for you if you are prioritizing the aging consumer.

The Boomers have enjoyed long and normal lives. As aging presents new and unanticipated developments, it's human nature to cope with and compensate for them in an effort to re-establish "normalcy." As they age and move forward, the normal that they once knew gets replaced by a "new normal." Reframing is an essential tool for realigning your brand's offering with a consumer's new normal. If you are true to the intent of a reframe, you often won't need to change your core product offering (the "art" in our analogy). Instead, you may only need to reframe it to alter its appearance and suitability for a new need in the new normal. If a picture is worth a thousand words, imagine how much it's worth with the right frame around it.

CHAPTER
SEVENTEEN

ENDURING MUTUAL RESPECT
Communicating authentically to get real results.

I was at a conference last year and I asked, as I often do, "How many of you are Boomers?" As usual, about 65% of the audience raised their hands. Then I asked, "How many of you are still actively working, spending money, consuming, doing what you have always done?" All of the Boomers' hands stayed up.

"OK. How many of you feel that the vast majority of advertising and marketing out there today understands you, respects you and brings you joy?" *All* of the hands went down.

I said, "Wait a second. You guys are the Baby Boomers. You consume 94% of consumer packaged goods and have 70% of the disposable income. You are a really big, important audience. You just said that none of the advertising out there understands you, respects you and brings you joy. Okay, so perhaps I was too ambitious in asking that question. I get that advertising sometimes doesn't bring you joy and maybe it doesn't always communicate that it loves you, but certainly all advertising must demonstrate on some level that it at least respects you, right? So let's have a show of hands, from those people who believe that the advertising out there today respects you." I couldn't get a single hand to go up.

Every year after the Super Bowl, befuddled Boomers ask me why they don't "get" the ads anymore. They'll go on and on about how they used to like the ads as much as the football, but now, they either don't understand them or don't appreciate the humor. I usually ask if they *really* want me to answer their question and of course, they insist. The answer is simple but painful – "They weren't created for you, they were created for the younger viewers." The reaction is one of outrage.

Nothing is more fundamental to the development of effective advertising than to demonstrate that you respect the consumer. This usually begins with respecting his or her intelligence. One of the greatest legends in our business – David Ogilvy – once quipped, "The consumer isn't a moron; she is your wife. You insult her intelligence if you assume that a mere slogan and a few vapid adjectives will persuade her to buy anything."[6]

Yet, there is a presumption in our business that aging people are of a less sound mind, and therefore easier to persuade using blunt tactics. In the case of the Boomers, this simply is not true.

Over the course of their media-consuming lifetimes, Boomers have developed the most sensitive BS detectors of any humans who have ever lived. Let's not forget, they were the original brand managers and helped to create the modern age of branding and consumerism. Boomers expect better from the brands that they admire and will reward them with the loyalty they *deserve*.

Respect also takes the form of authenticity. The ultimate form of engagement is to create the type of advertising that gets consumers to identify with your brand because they perceive that you understand them. How often have you heard people say, "Now there's a brand that gets it!"? What they're really saying is, "There's a brand that gets *me*!" The brands that do this consistently well are the brands that work hardest to get a genuine understanding of the consumer that is expressed authentically in advertising.

One of my all-time favorite campaigns belongs to Budweiser, my brand of beer for life. Its memorable "For all you do, this Bud's for you" campaign enjoyed a good long run from 1979 to 1994. Budweiser clearly understood who drank their beer – hardworking men – and it saluted them for their patriotic work ethic. There isn't a hardworking person out there who doesn't feel underappreciated, and when it comes time to reward themselves with an ice-cold beer, what brand could be better than the brand that appreciates all that they do? Authenticity at its best.

Finally, respect takes the form of talking one's language. Have you ever walked into a store in Europe, knowing that there's more than a good chance that the shopkeeper speaks English, only to be brushed off for not being capable enough of speaking the native tongue? Just because you are advertising in English doesn't mean you are speaking a consumer's language, just like the Boomers who don't "get" the ads in the Super Bowl. They are failing to comprehend the ads because they were written in a younger consumer's language. In this case, the language takes the form of slang vocabulary, pop-culture iconography and genres of humor specific to youth.

Does this mean that today's Super Bowl ads are bad? Of course not. Instead, we use them as an example to communicate two relevant points about advertising to Boomers. First, to illustrate that they still expect – rightfully or wrongfully – advertisers to prioritize them and to speak to them. After all, if you look at the incredible growth in the NFL property from 1950 (thirteen teams) to now (thirty-two teams), it has to be attributed to the Boomers who drove television ratings, attended games and bought closets full of team attire. Indeed, it was the Boomers who made the Super Bowl super, so why shouldn't they expect to still be the focus of this great sporting and advertising event?

Second, that there's a risk in alienating the Boomers – in any advertising medium – if you don't demonstrate that you respect them. Budweiser has been brilliant in walking the fine line of appealing to youth while still speaking to the Boomers who still drink a lot of beer. They can get as youth-wonky as they want in their Super Bowl ads, but the fact that I can always expect a smart and entertaining Clydesdale ad says that Budweiser still appreciates "all that I do" by buying their beer year in and year out.

I continue to use the Budweiser example because I'm a Boomer and it's a brand I'm deeply loyal to – there's a case study in here somewhere. With the proliferation of beer brands and craft brews, there has been plenty of attractive temptation, but I have stayed true to the red, white and blue beer. The real reason for this loyalty beyond reason is that Budweiser has stayed true to itself. It has done a brilliant job in managing its brand equity over time and in keeping it relevant to me as I have changed over time. This gets back to our discussion of generational marketing. Budweiser has apparently marketed to my core personal values, values that have remained unchanged as my age and life stages have changed. I value hard work, patriotism, quality and permanence, values that are spot-on with what Budweiser has also stood for over time.

If Budweiser is an example of my enduring loyalty – because it is a brand that has been loyal to me – Levi's is an example of a brand for which my loyalty has lapsed. I wore Levi's 501s for forty years because, not unlike Budweiser, the brand's values were similar to mine: hard work, patriotism, quality and permanence. My impression of the brand's current advertising – subjective though it may be – is that it depicts people who don't work, vote or pay taxes, and wear jeans that are made overseas and therefore don't last as long as they used to – all characteristics that are near opposites of my personal value system. It should come as no surprise that I opted out of this system of brand beliefs for another brand – J.L. Powell – that is more in sync with what I value and respect.

In my heart, I still *love* Levi's, but I can't get over the fact that they lost *respect* for me. Love without respect is not enough to sustain loyalty.

Let's face it. I grew too old for Levi's. Levi's is a smart brand, and it made a strategic choice to focus on youth via the eighteen to thirty-four target, and it will sell a lot of denim to these folks. That said, it chose eighteen to thirty-four versus Boomers because it believed it had to choose one or the other but not both. This is the *either/or* dilemma that is the by-product of a mass marketing model that has too much inertia around its traditional targeting model.

What better brand to participate in The Old Rush than a brand that was born in the Gold Rush? The Boomers practically invented Levi's and drove years and years of phenomenal growth with loyalty like my forty years' worth. The distinctly American values of Levi's – inspired by the Gold Rush – were brilliantly in sync with a patriotic post-war youth looking for a proletarian statement of independence. Why would you let such extended loyalty lapse if there was a way to still speak to Boomers who still love blue jeans and will be wearing them more often as their daily leisure time expands? The Old Rush is the new opportunity to get it right all over again.

If Levi's reintroduced its 501 Originals as *our* originals, it wouldn't take much for Boomers to rekindle their love. A gesture of respect, combined with gratitude for years of loyalty? What a great fit. Loyalty only perseveres when respect perseveres, and as we've said throughout this book, Boomer loyalty is not something that can be taken for granted simply because it has endured for so long. To use an analogy, think of loyalty as a car that runs on a tank of respect. The tank has been filled over the years through great brand experiences that grow and reinforce respect. As those positive, respect-building brand experiences diminish or go away altogether, the level of respect in the tank goes down and begins to approach empty. Just as a car will run until the fuel runs out and it dies, such is the same for respect. It's there one day and then it's not, and loyalty comes to a halt.

To continue the analogy, the Boomers have been gradually exiting the eighteen to forty-nine cohort for years. If eighteen to forty-nine is the Boomer fuel tank, it's been approaching empty for some time now. What is your strategy for filling the tank once it is completely empty in 2014? There's a good chance that my Budweiser and Levi's stories provide some answers. There's likely to be enough residual love that can be activated again with a simple gesture of respect. Join The Old Rush and earn back some of the hard-won loyalty with a little respect for the aging consumer.

CHAPTER EIGHTEEN

BRAND BELONGING
*Going beyond loyalty for relationships
that last a lifetime.*

lmost every day I hear someone rue the fact that "loyalty is dead." Most often, this line is spoken in regard to employment and reflects that, in general, companies are now much less loyal to their employees. By the same token, employees are less loyal to their employers. Is this a reflection of the changing nature of business relationships, or are we seeing a widening of the gap between employer and employee values? It's probably a combination of both.

If employer/employee loyalty is dead or dying, what is the state of brand loyalty? In answering this question, we will do so as marketers who value a sustained relationship between brands and buyers because it's less expensive than a perpetual recruiting trial. Do consumers benefit from the dynamic of loyalty? Not really. They benefit from a sustained positive experience with brands that serve them well, but they do not derive a direct benefit from loyalty itself. Net, consumers aren't motivated by the prospect of loyalty like we are, and, in truth, proliferation of choice serves them better than loyalty.

So, is the brand loyalty that marketers covet dead? No, but it is fair to say that it's under siege. The fundamental driver of the erosion of loyalty is the proliferation of equally attractive choices. In turn, equally attractive choices are the by-product of the increasing commoditization of product categories. If all of the products are seen as being similar in quality and benefit, lowest price becomes the most meaningful differentiator in a world of otherwise identical choices.

I majored in economics in college. The most basic of economic theories at the time spoke to the importance of "pure competition" in growing and sustaining a marketplace. Some of the requirements for pure competition were many buyers/ many sellers, supply equal to demand, full information and a lack of collusion. What seemed to be only theory at the time has now become reality, thanks to technology. The technology behind e-tailing has created purely competitive marketplaces that directly link the economy's many buyers and sellers, along with price comparison apps that allow customers to benefit from having full information before making an educated purchase. From a consumer standpoint, technology-led commoditization is beneficial, as it drives value – quite the opposite for large marketers who are dependent on brick-and-mortar distribution and need to drive differentiation to create loyalty.

Another driver of commoditization and increased choice is the significant improvement in the quality of private label or store brands. The balance of power in the manufacturer-retailer relationship has shifted dramatically since the advent of powerful retailers such as Walmart. Manufacturers, lacking the leverage they once had, must now compete head-on with their customers' own brands. Loyalty is indeed under siege.

In military strategy, if you are under siege, you can: (1) dig in and defend your territory; (2) retreat and regroup to fight another day; or (3) relocate to higher ground to seize back the advantage. If you're a marketer, options 1 and 2 are usually intensive and costly endeavors. Ideally, it's best to move to higher ground to enjoy a position that your competitors can't readily attain.

In my years at Saatchi & Saatchi, we espoused a belief about branding that was called Lovemarks. This was an attempt to create a new, higher level of loyalty to rise above the traditional level of loyalty that was under siege. It spoke to a type of loyalty – "loyalty beyond reason" – that was theoretically less impervious to switching.

That cutting-edge theory of loyalty is now nearly a decade old, and in those years we have witnessed unrelenting pressure on loyalty, accelerated by a lingering global recession that prompted unprecedented levels of value-driven brand switching. At the same time, the Most Valuable Generation™ of consumers – and arguably the most loyal – aged out of advertising's eighteen to forty-nine sweet spot. There's never been a better time for a new philosophy and approach to brand loyalty.

The Old Rush will see the advent of a new model of brand loyalty, which we call Brand Belonging. One way to understand brand belonging is to better understand what brand loyalty is not.

Brand loyalty is essentially a measurement of sustained purchase frequency – it measures repeat transactions. It is fundamentally transactional, and it is not a measurement or indication of the consumer's level of engagement with the brand.

Ironically, we live in a modern age of marketing in which we often speak about consumer engagement as if it were some new, more valuable way of reaching prospects. As long as we still covet brand loyalty, success will be defined by transactions, not some deeper level of true engagement that drives enduring loyalty.

Brand belonging is a philosophy that begins where loyalty leaves off – engagement – and goes further to a level of relationship that is nearly permanent. Loyalty simply means a consistent and dedicated pattern of choosing a brand. Belonging says the brand is so meaningful to me that I have become one with the brand. The brand is essential to my being. It defines me. It is part of me. I cannot live without it.

Here are some examples of existing brands that are enjoying the benefits of brand belonging without having explicitly attempted to create a level of engagement beyond loyalty. They are also brands that Boomers will tell you they "belong" to.

Harley-Davidson is not a motorcycle, it's an ethos. When you buy a Harley, you don't just buy a means of transportation, you join a community. To own a Harley is to belong to Harley – it is instant kinship. Harley riders recognize each other on the road and form instant friendships based purely on the respect and trust derived from ownership. While Harley nurtures the heritage and ethos that it has built up around its bikes, the vibrancy of the Harley ecosphere is equally driven by the passion of the riders who are members of the distinctive Harley clan. Harley and its owners co-perpetuate belonging.

American Express articulates belonging as membership. You're not simply a cardholder, you're a cardmember. I take special pride in the fact that my card reads "member since 1981," and I have no intention whatsoever to divorce myself from this long marriage. "Membership has its privileges" not only reinforces that I'm a "member" of American Express, it also conveys a private set of conveniences, advantages and recognitions bestowed upon me for my extended loyalty. Why pay with a simple debit card when I can pay with my American Express card? What's beautiful about this is that I don't really get any significant privileges, but I feel as if I do, which is all that matters. "Member since 1981." Behold the power of Brand Belonging.

Loyalty programs, done well, can become belonging programs. In my mind and heart, I am not just loyal to Delta Airlines – I belong to Delta. So profound is my loyalty that I will literally opt for a higher-priced connecting flight on Delta over a cheaper, direct flight with another carrier. The others are just carriers, but Delta is my airline.

With the nearly universal dislike of air travel, how could something so wonderful happen? Simply put, Delta has found a way to personalize a commoditized experience for me. As proof that the little things can make a big difference – especially in a low-satisfaction category – it brings me great joy every time I board a plane and the flight attendant says "Hello Mr. Hubbell. Welcome back – thanks for your miles and your loyalty." How much does it cost them to say that? Nothing. How much does it mean to me? Priceless. Oh, and by the way, I'm a business traveler, which means that I fly frequently and frequently pay full fare. They love me, and I love them. We belong together.

Like loyalty, Belonging is not accomplished overnight, but its benefits are longer lasting. Over the years, Harley has put a lot of research and development into new bikes to stay attuned to the needs of its brand clan and to deepen their sense of belonging. One of their areas of focus has been Touring Bikes – bikes that are comfortable and sturdy enough for long-distance travel. One of Harley's innovations was the "softail frame," which, as the name might imply, has a suspension system that makes the ride softer on the rider's tailbone. More-comfortable bikes are what aging Boomers are likely to be looking for as they head out on the highway in numbers in the coming years.

Lou Pritchett, a legendary P&G salesman and change agent, once defined the objective of loyalty as one of "keeping the costs of switching high." It's a very interesting way of thinking about loyalty at a time when most think that success lies in keeping costs low to keep prices low. The cost that Pritchett was speaking to is the value that the consumer associates with the benefits of the brand. If you can keep the value of the brand experience higher than the competition, the consumer will have a disincentive to switch because doing so will result in a forfeiture of value.

Brand Belonging is a relationship-based strategy that perpetuates loyalty by keeping the costs of switching high. Once you've had a taste of the "good life," it's hard to go back. Finally, in a day and age in which social media advocacy plays such an important role in shaping brand reputations, having consumers feel that they belong to your brand is money in the bank. They aren't just Facebook friends, they're part of a club – Belongers are the ultimate brand ambassadors.

Thriving in The Old Rush is all about striving to do things differently. That obviously begins with targeting the highly valuable aging consumer, but as we've learned, it also requires overcoming philosophical barriers to change and embracing new approaches like generational marketing and Brand Belonging.

There was nothing ordinary about the Gold Rush, but the rewards were extraordinary enough to justify the risks. Comparatively, there is very little risk in The Old Rush if you have a smart plan and you execute it intelligently. In most cases, the Boomers have already had some type of positive relationship with your brand, so your challenge is really only one of rekindling the relationship. There is nothing more valuable than your brand, and there is no generation of consumers more valuable than the Boomers. Opportunities like this are few.

The inherent theme of The Old Rush is speed. The new

imperative in business is fast growth, and with the speed at which commoditization is taking place, it has never been more critical to identify quickly a truly differentiated fast growth strategy. From our vantage point in marketing, there is no other fast growth opportunity as enticing as the aging consumer, and the way forward is relatively simple.

As you ponder your alternatives, I'll leave you with an inspirational thought from my own experience in founding BoomAgers. Not unlike a '49er, I knew from the outset that there was massive potential in digging for gold where no one else was. The logic of it all made great sense but logic alone seldom launches dreams. What I needed most, I still lacked – that last small shred of courage to take the first step. As with great ideas in the ad business, you never know where they're going to come from, and they almost never come from the place you look for them. I had a hunch that the "shot of courage" that I needed to start my own company would also come from an unexpected place at an unexpected time. Not in my wildest dreams would I have imagined that it would have come from a child's book while reading to my seven-year-old son Teddy at bedtime.

Leave it to Dr. Seuss to have the prescription I needed. How many times before had I read *Oh, the places you'll go!* ? – a wonderful book with cute words and that trademark Seuss cadence, but on this particular reading, it was as if all of the words had been changed and he was talking to me!

I was the one that had brains in my head and feet in my shoes and it was up to me to choose which road to use. If Seuss's kid could go places, then surely this grown-up could too. The moment that bedtime story was over, I was on my way, and I've never looked back. I haven't moved any mountains yet, but if and when it makes sense to do so, I'm reasonably confident that it's possible.

So now it's your turn go to the places you'll go. You'll have lots of roads to choose, but if your destination is The Old Rush, the direction to head in is very straightforward. You'll need to cross some mountains on the way there, but if you pack enough confidence, you'll be able to move them. Good luck and safe journeys.

AFTERWORD
THE LEGACY OF THE OLD RUSH

Jane Pauley and I share a similar passion for our generation and are in different but influential positions to effect positive change – Jane by way of her iconic reputation, the Boomer-driven *Life Reimagined* AARP television series and her new book *Your Life Calling: Reimagining the Rest of Your Life,* and me by way of BoomAgers' mission and relationship with some of the world's top marketers. She and I were musing a bit when I asked her what she thought the legacy of our generation should be. Many of us Boomers were the children of the Greatest Generation, who were prepared to make the ultimate sacrifice to preserve our country's way of life. Their legacy is poignant and clear.

But when you consider the massive, unprecedented size of the Baby Boomer generation, and you witness their historic ability to transform the culture around them, it's somewhat perplexing that their legacy is nowhere in sight. With such potency, one can't help but wonder what the possibilities might be for our generation. We celebrate the fact that our age hasn't stopped us, and we claim that we're only just getting started, so where is it we want to go and what will we do to benefit those that will follow us?

I looked at Jane and I said, "We're entitled to dream, right?" She replied, "We always have, so why should we stop now?" Amen. So here's my dream for our generation: I aspire that we will act in a way that creates an American culture that respects its elders the way other prominent nations do, and in the way that our own growing majority-minority does.

If we're honest with ourselves, we're the ones who created this phenomenon – or at least perpetuated it – so it's our responsibility to address it. Throughout our young lives, we embraced the old folks stereotype, in advertising, entertainment and in our own conduct. We stigmatized aging while celebrating our youth.

Now the tables have been turned – we have become them. I for one don't believe that the Boomers will tolerate being treated as old people the way we ourselves treated old people when we were young. Call it a double standard, but we are where we are and there's no reversing time.

While we can't reverse time, we do still have time to make a difference. Many of us are still in jobs and positions that afford us access to potent mechanisms of change, chief among them being the media. If we act now, our dream might just become a reality. If we wait, the window may close on us forever. It's imponderable that a generation of this magnitude and wherewithal might fail to bequeath a positive legacy to others.

Our opportunity is here now, and it is The Old Rush. I urge you all to act to make a difference. To create products that bring new innovation to old age; to paint images of aging that are as aspirational as youth; to treat age as a source of status gained through the mastery of life; to respect the Boomers' intelligence as you respect your own, and to believe that your actions, from a position of influence, can create an exponential amount of goodwill.

So let us head off to The Old Rush together with the assurance of knowing that even if we don't find gold we will most certainly discover the richness of trying to make a difference.

I expect to pass through this world but once.
Any good, therefore, that I can do or any kindness
I can show to any fellow creature,
let me do it now.
Let me not defer or neglect it
for I shall not pass this way again.

(THIS IS GENERALLY CREDITED TO STEPHEN GRELLET,
BUT WITHOUT PROVEN ATTRIBUTION)

RECOMMENDED READING

For those of you who want to take a deeper dive into any of the themes and topics explored in *The Old Rush*, here is a select list of some of my favorite sources of research and thinking.

Andersen, Kurt. *Heyday*. New York: Random House Trade Paperbacks, Reprint edition, 2007. (A well-researched novel set during the Gold Rush.)

Bach, Sharon, and Ken Ostermann. *The Legend Begins: Harley-Davidson Motorcycles, 1903–1969*. Milwaukee, WI: Harley-Davidson, Inc., 1993.

Brands, H.W. *The Age of Gold: The California Gold Rush and The New American Dream*. New York: Anchor, 2003.

Cheung, Edward. *Baby Boomers, Generation X and Social Cycles, Volume 1: North American Long-waves*. Toronto: Longwave Press, Expanded edition, 2007.

Clurman, Ann, and J. Walker Smith. *Generation Ageless: How Baby Boomers Are Changing the Way We Live Today . . . And They're Just Getting Started*. New York: HarperBusiness, 2007.

Dalzell, Frederick, Davis Dyer, and Rowena Olegario. *Rising Tide: Lessons from 165 Years of Brand Building at Procter & Gamble*. Boston: Harvard Business Review Press, 2004.

Dychtwald, Ken. *Age Power: How the 21st Century Will Be Ruled by the New Old*. New York: Tarcher/Penguin, 2000.

Ehrlich, Paul R. *The Population Bomb*. Cutchogue, NY: Buccaneer Books, Reprint edition, 1995.

Fendley, Alison. *Saatchi & Saatchi: the Inside Story.* Collingdale, PA: Diane Publishing Co., 1995.

Freedman, Marc. *Prime Time: How Baby Boomers Will Revolutionize Retirement and Transform America.* New York: Public Affairs/Perseus, 2002.

Foot, David, Brian Gable, and Daniel Stoffman. *Boom, Bust and Echo: Profiting from the Demographic Shift in the 21st century.* Toronto: Stoddart, 2001.

Gillon, Steve. *Boomer Nation: The Largest and Richest Generation Ever, and How It Changed America.* New York: Free Press, 2004.

Heath, Chip, and Dan Heath. *Made to Stick.* New York: Random House, 2007.

Howe, Neil, and William Strauss. *Generations: The History of America's Future, 1584 to 2069.* New York: William Morrow & Company, 1991.

Hower, Ralph. *The History of an Advertising Agency: N. W. Ayer & Son.* Cambridge: Harvard University Press, Revised edition, 1949.

Hudson, Frederic M. *The Adult Years: Mastering the Art of Self-Renewal.* San Francisco: Jossey-Bass, Revised edition, 1999.

Ibarra, Herminia. *Working Identity: Unconventional Strategies for Reinventing Your Career.* Boston: Harvard Business School Press, 2004.

Jones, Landon. *Great Expectations: America & the Baby Boom Generation.* Charleston, SC: BookSurge Publishing/ Amazon, 2008.

Kennedy, Dan S., and Chip Kessler. *No B.S. Guide to Marketing to Leading-Edge Boomers and Seniors.* Irvine, CA: Entrepreneur Press, 2012.

Lafley, A.G. and Roger L. Martin. *Playing to Win: How Strategy Really Works.* Boston: Harvard Business Review Press, 2013

Lafley, A.G. and Ram Charan. *The Game Changer: How Every Leader Can Drive Everyday Innovation.* New York: Crown Publishing, 2008

Leider, Richard J., and Alan M. Webber. *Life Reimagined: Discovering Your New Life Possibilities.* San Francisco: Berrett-Koehler Publishers, 2013.

Martin, John, and Matt Thornhill. *Boomer Consumer: Ten New Rules for Marketing to America's Largest, Wealthiest and Most Influential Group.* Great Falls, VA: LINX Corp, 2007.

Michener, James A. *Alaska.* New York: Fawcett Crest, 1989. (This book includes a gripping fiction-based-on-fact account of the Klondike Gold Rush, which had similar dynamics to the California Gold Rush.)

O'Hara, Christopher B. *Great American Beer: 50 Brands That Shaped the 20th Century.* New York: Clarkson Potter/Crown Publishing/Random House, 2006.

Owram, Doug. *Born at the Right Time.* Toronto: University of Toronto Press, 1997.

Pauley, Jane. *Your Life Calling: Reimagining the Rest of Your Life.* New York: Simon & Schuster, 2014.

Rosenblatt, Roger. *Rules for Aging.* New York: Harcourt, 2001. (Award-winning essayist, journalist, author, playwright and teacher Roger Rosenblatt shares some of his observations about aging and gives memorable advice.)

Smead, Howard. *Don't Trust Anyone Over Thirty: The First Four Decades of the Baby Boom.* Bloomington, IN: iUniverse, 2000.

Sullivan, James. *Jeans: A Cultural History of an American Icon.* New York: Gotham/Penguin, 2007.

Walker, Michael C. *Marketing to Seniors.* Miami: 1st Book Library, 2nd edition, 2002.

Wallace, Paul. *Agequake: Riding the Demographic Rollercoaster Shaking Business, Finance, and Our World* Boston: Nicholas Brealey Publishing, 2001.

NOTES

PART ONE

1. BoomAgers and The Nielsen Company, "Introducing Boomers: Marketing's Most Valuable Generation," *The Nielsen Company*, August 6, 2012, http://www.nielsen.com/us/en/reports/2012/introducing-boomers--marketing-s-most-valuable-generation.html.

2. BoomAgers and The Nielsen Company, "Introducing Boomers" and Doug Anderson, "How Old Is Old: The Global Impact of an Aging World," *The Nielsen Company*, February 11, 2011, http://www.nielsen.com/us/en/newswire/2011/how-old-is-old-the-global-impact-of-an-aging-world.html.

3. BoomAgers and The Nielsen Company, "Introducing Boomers."

4. D'vera Cohn and Paul Taylor, "Baby Boomers Approach 65 – Glumly," *Pew Research Social & Demographic Trends* (2010), http://pewresearch.org/pubs/1834/baby-boomers-old-age-downbeat-pessimism.

5. "Most Middle-Aged Adults are Rethinking Retirement Plans," *Pew Research Social & Demographic Trends*, May 28, 2009, http://www.pewsocialtrends.org/2009/05/28/most-middle-aged-adults-are-rethinking-retirement-plans/.

6. BoomAgers and The Nielsen Company, "Introducing Boomers," and Anderson, "How Old Is Old."

7. BoomAgers and The Nielsen Company, "Introducing Boomers."

8. Cohn and Taylor, "Baby Boomers Approach 65 – Glumly."

9. *Id.*

10. "Calculators," *Social Security Administration*, accessed February 6, 2014, http://www.ssa.gov/planners/benefitcalculators.htm.

11. Shelly Emling, "Baby Boomer Entrepreneurs Take More Risks Than Generation Y," *The Huffington Post*, February 27,

2013, http://www.huffingtonpost.com/2013/02/27/baby-boomers-entrepreneurs-more-entrepreneurial-than-generation-y_n_2767195.html.

12. "Beyond 50.05: A Report to the Nation on Livable Communities: Creating Environments for Successful Aging," *AARP,* accessed February 6, 2014, http://assets.aarp.org/rgcenter/il/beyond_50_communities.pdf.

13. Anne Tergesen, "For Second Careers, A Leap of Faith," *The Wall Street Journal,* May 19, 2013, http://on.wsj.com/12F6d5o.

PART TWO

1. "California Gold Rush," *Wikipedia, The Free Encyclopedia,* accessed January 24, 2014, http://en.wikipedia.org/wiki/California_Gold_Rush.

2. "The Gold Rush of 1849," *History.com,* accessed February 5, 2014, http://www.history.com/topics/gold-rush-of-1849.

3. Chauncey L. Canfield, "Diary of a Forty-Niner," *openlibrary.org.*

4. Levi Strauss & Co., "Our Story," accessed February 5, 2014, http://www.levistrauss.com/our-story/#heritage-timeline.

5. Nordstrom, "Company History," accessed February 5, 2014, http://shop.nordstrom.com/c/company-history.

6. "History of San Francisco," *Wikipedia, The Free Encyclopedia,* accessed January 30, 2014, http://en.wikipedia.org/wiki/History_of_San_Francisco.

7. Judith Downey, "Consequences of California Mania: Nantucket and the Whaling Industry," *Nantucket Historical Association,* vol. 48, no. 3 (Summer 1999), pp. 25–26.

8. Barbara Maranzani, "8 Things You May Not Know About the California Gold Rush," *History.com,* January 24, 2014, http://www.history.com/news/8-things-you-may-not-know-about-the-california-gold-rush.

9. "Samuel Brannan," *Wikipedia, The Free Encyclopedia,* accessed February 5, 2014, http://en.wikipedia.org/wiki/Samuel_Brannan.

10. "Central Pacific Railroad," *Wikipedia, The Free Encyclopedia,* accessed February 17, 2014, http://en.wikipedia.org/wiki/Central_Pacific_Railroad.

11. "Wells Fargo History," accessed February 5, 2014, http://www.wellsfargohistory.com/.

12. Maranzani, "8 Things You May Not Know About the California Gold Rush."

13. The Nantucket Coffee Connection, *N Magazine* (The Nantucket Magazine), May 2013, p. 100.

14. Vardis Fisher & Opal Laurel Holmes, *Gold Rushes and Mining Camps of the Early American West.* Caldwell, Idaho: The Caxton Printers, Ltd., 1968.

15. "The Gold Rush of 1849," *History.com*, accessed February 5, 2014, http://www.history.com/topics/gold-rush-of-1849.

16. Steve Wiegand, "The California Gold Rush: An Era Remembered," *The Sacramento Bee*, January 18, 1998, http://www.calgoldrush.com/part1/01overview.html.

17. *Id.*

PART THREE

1. BoomAgers and The Nielsen Company, "Introducing Boomers."

2. *Id.*

3. "Paint by Number," *Wikipedia, The Free Encyclopedia,* accessed November 13, 2014, http://en.wikipedia.org/wiki/Paint_by_number.

4. "Growing Old in America: Expectations vs. Reality," *Pew Research*, June 29, 2009, http://www.pewsocialtrends.org/2009/06/29/growing-old-in-america-expectations-vs-reality/2/. In 2014, the Boomers range in age from fifty to sixty-eight.

5. *Id.*

6. David Oglivy, *Confessions of An Advertising Man* (London: Southbank Publishing, 2004).

ABOUT BOOMAGERS
THE BOOMAGERS MANIFESTO

BoomAgers is the first modern creative services and marketing communications agency for the *Age of Aging*. At BoomAgers, we believe that aging is the most potent global power trend of the next twenty years. No other force will have a more profound impact on global economies, societies and cultures than aging.

Founded by Peter Hubbell in 2012, BoomAgers has grown exponentially from its humble beginnings with a single client and one part-time employee. From the beginning, BoomAgers has been purpose-built to deliver unique expertise and insight into the aging consumer. Our insights, strategies and creativity enable both established global brands and emerging companies to capture the full value of the massive but underleveraged aging marketplace.

We believe that "it takes one to know one," and we are proud to be Baby Boomers. We take it as a core truth that there is joy in aging, and we have the passion and experience to express elemental human truths in ways that make brands and products irresistible. We are Boomers dedicated to Boomers – *the new B2B*.

We believe that "the secret to success is knowing the secrets," and as Boomers, our team has accumulated years of invaluable experience in top roles at major agencies.

We've been there and done that. We know where the creative bull's-eye is, and we get right to the point.

We are practical pioneers. We are motivated by a collective

dissatisfaction with the way things are typically done at big ad agencies. We have our priorities straight, and we put the consumer first because the consumer is the ultimate arbiter – that's who buys our clients' products and services. We also believe that sameness in advertising never works. So, we work differently – a process that starts by attracting and inspiring the best people in the business.

We believe that innovation is different from frantic change. Innovation is what you do to solve your hardest problems. We believe that the hardest problem for marketers today is generating fast growth in a slow-growth market. We know from experience that fast growth is created by doing business where no one else is, or doing business differently. We are convinced that targeting the underleveraged, aging consumer accomplishes both.

We are the Boomer experts. We are your opportunity.

BEYOND
THE WRITTEN WORD

Authors who speak to you face to face.

Discover LID Speakers, a service that enables businesses to have direct and interactive contact with the best ideas brought to their own sector by the most outstanding creators of business thinking.

- A network specialising in business speakers, making it easy to find the most suitable candidates.

- A website with full details and videos, so you know exactly who you're hiring.

- A forum packed with ideas and suggestions about the most interesting and cutting-edge issues.

- A place where you can make direct contact with the best in international speakers.

- The only speakers' bureau backed up by the expertise of an established business book publisher.

LIDspeakers
.com
Sure value.